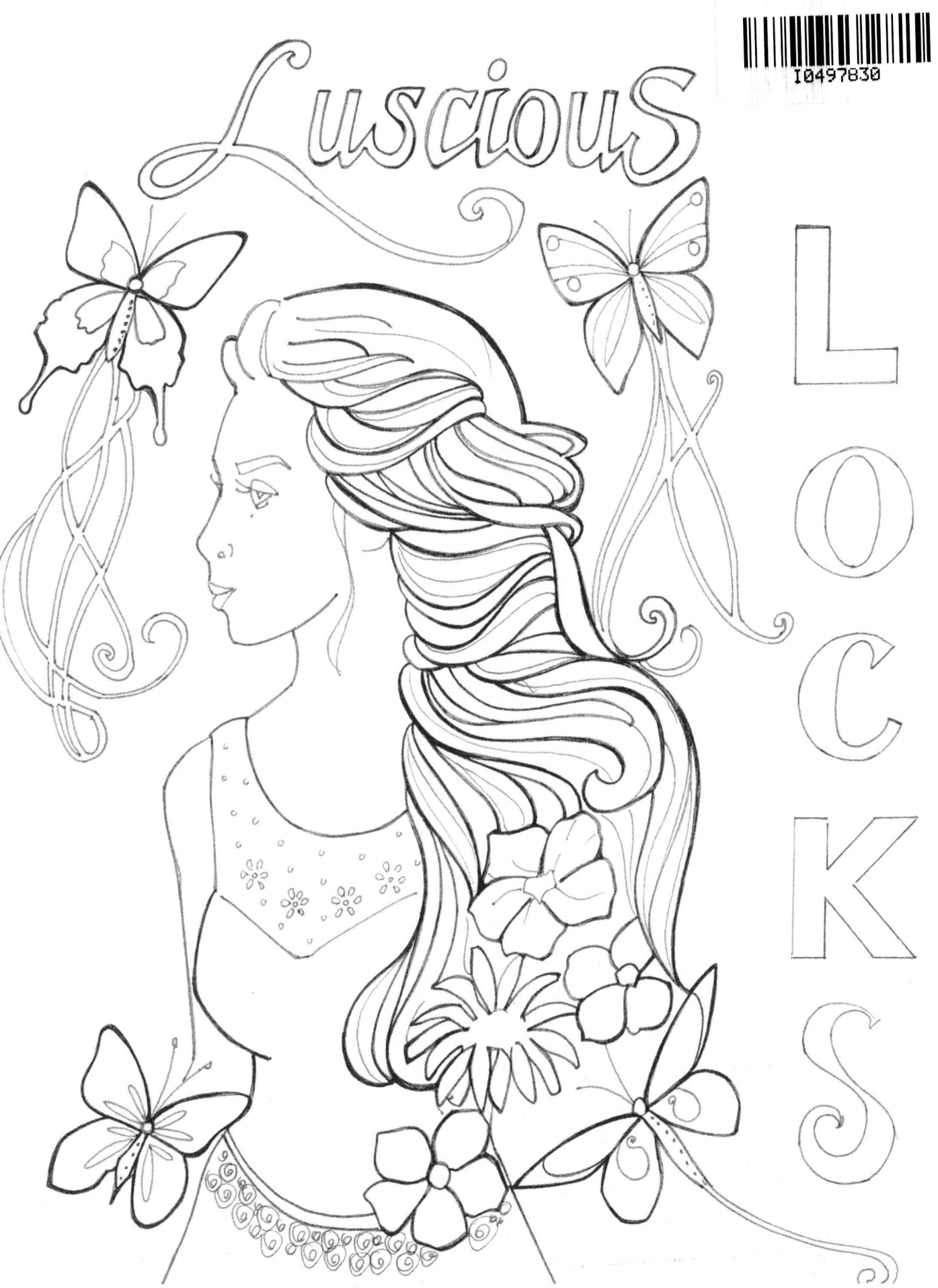

All images ©2021 Laurie Kapalka. All rights reserved. No part of this publication is to be reproduced, distributed, or transmiitted in any form or by any means, including photocopying, recording or other electronic or mechanical methods without prior written permission of the artist. Photocopying is permitted for PERSONAL USE ONLY. Absolutely no commercial use of any image is permitted.

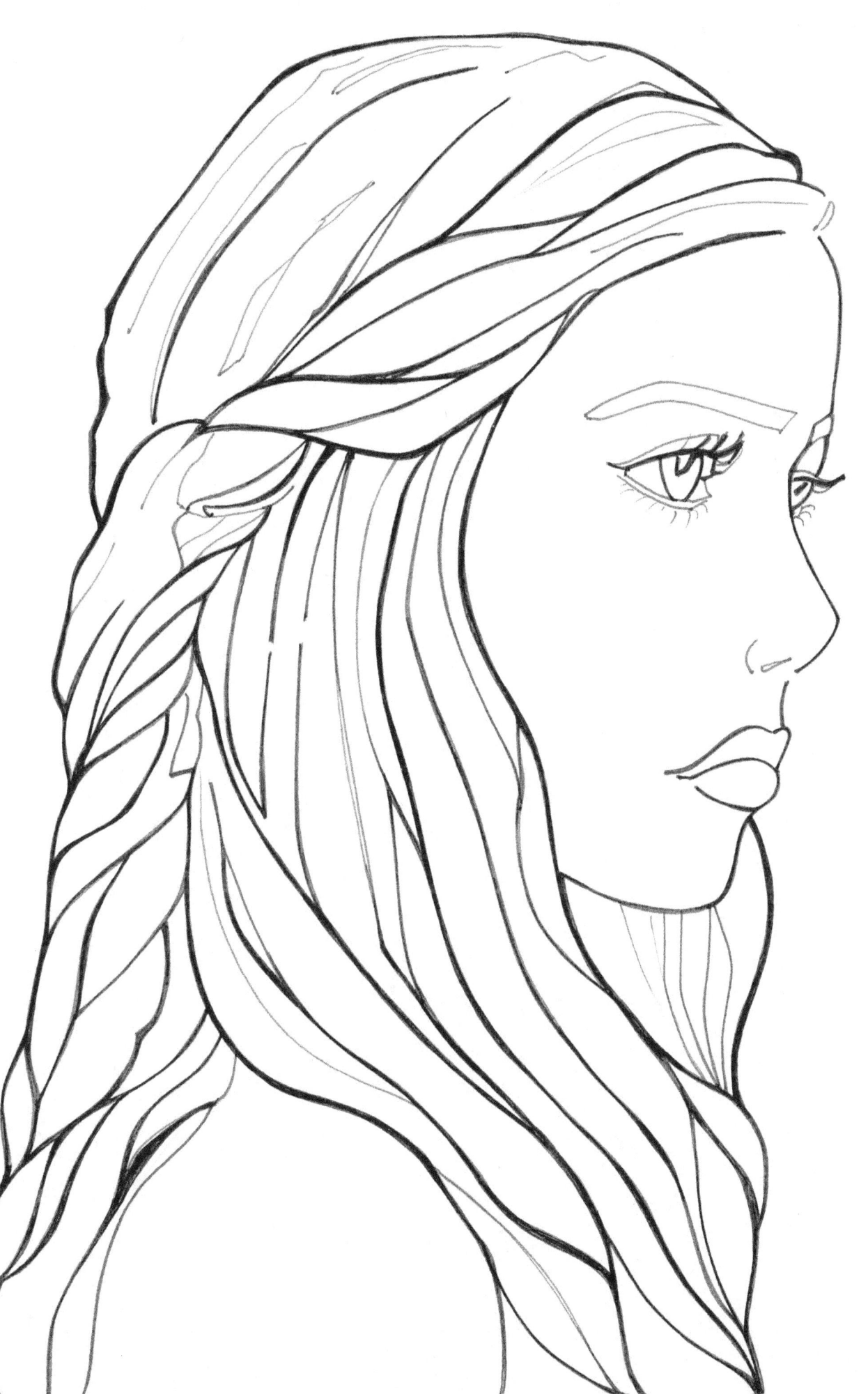

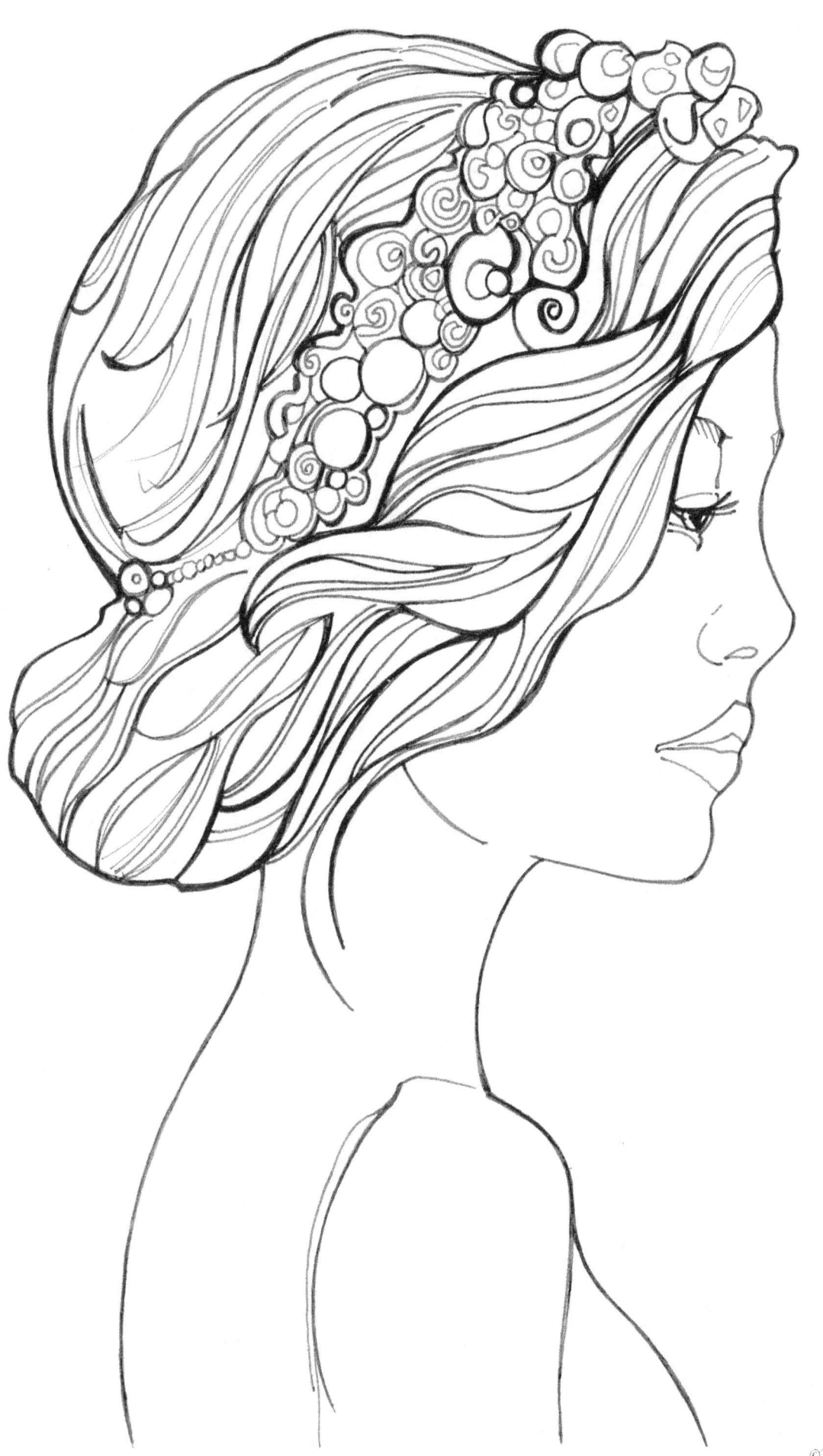

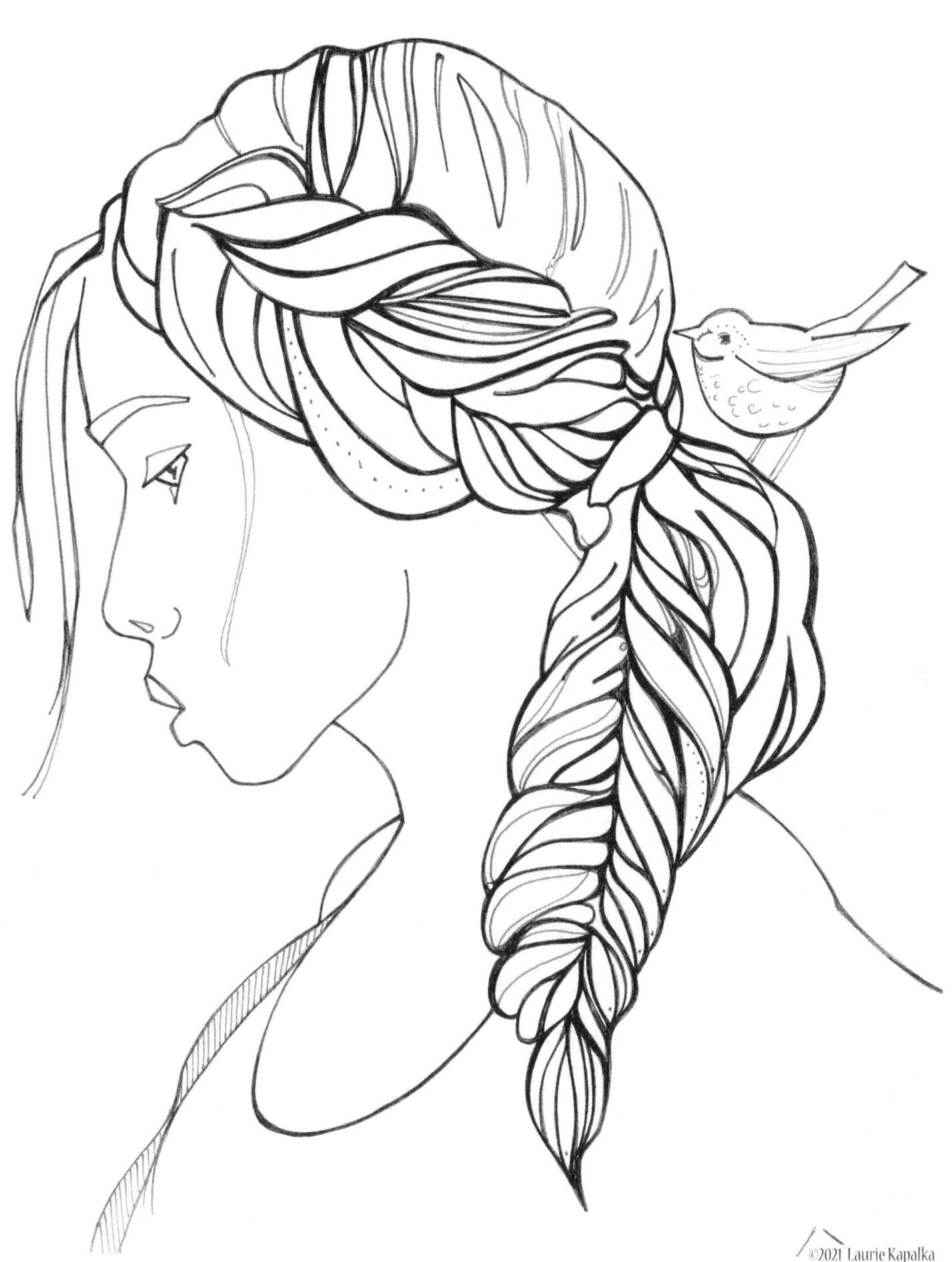

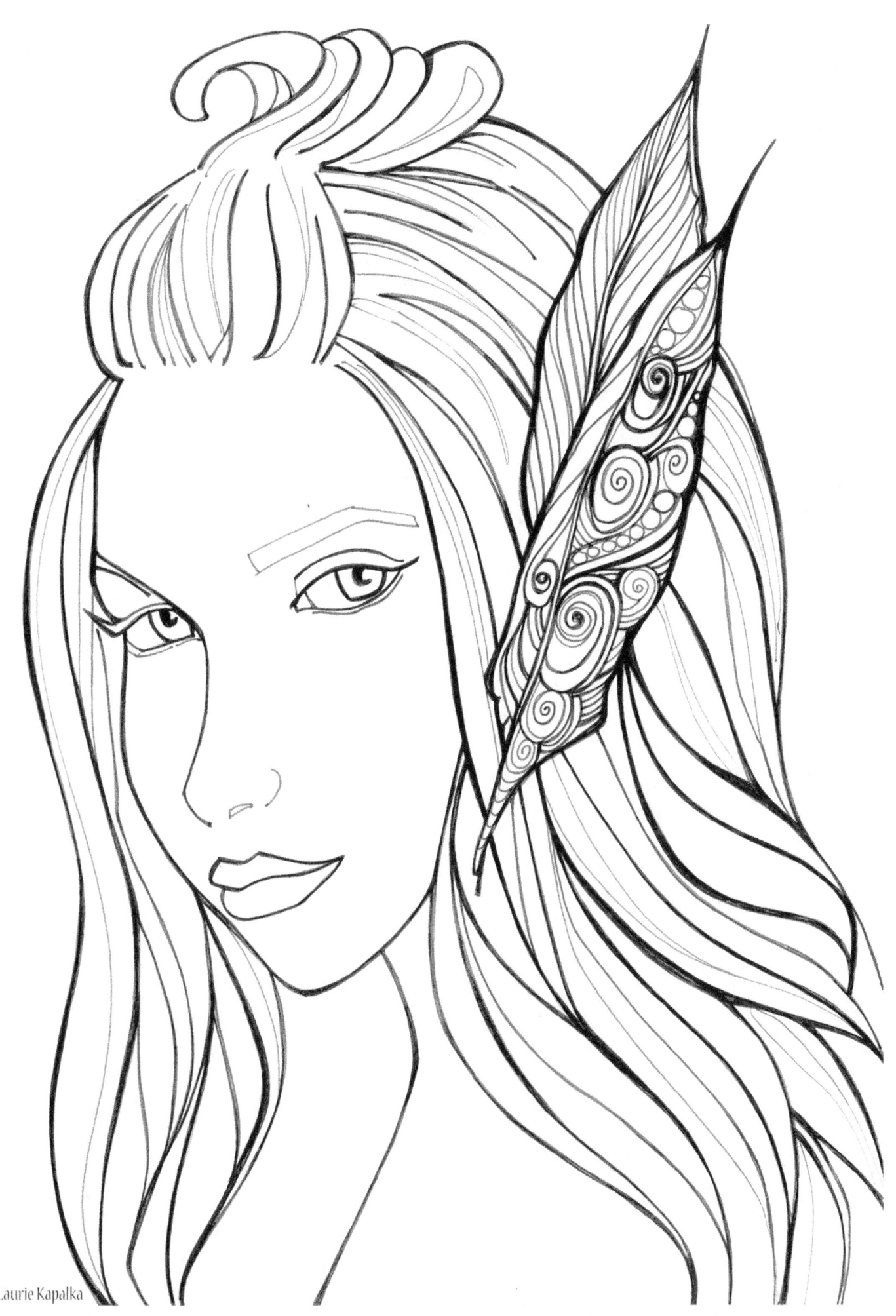

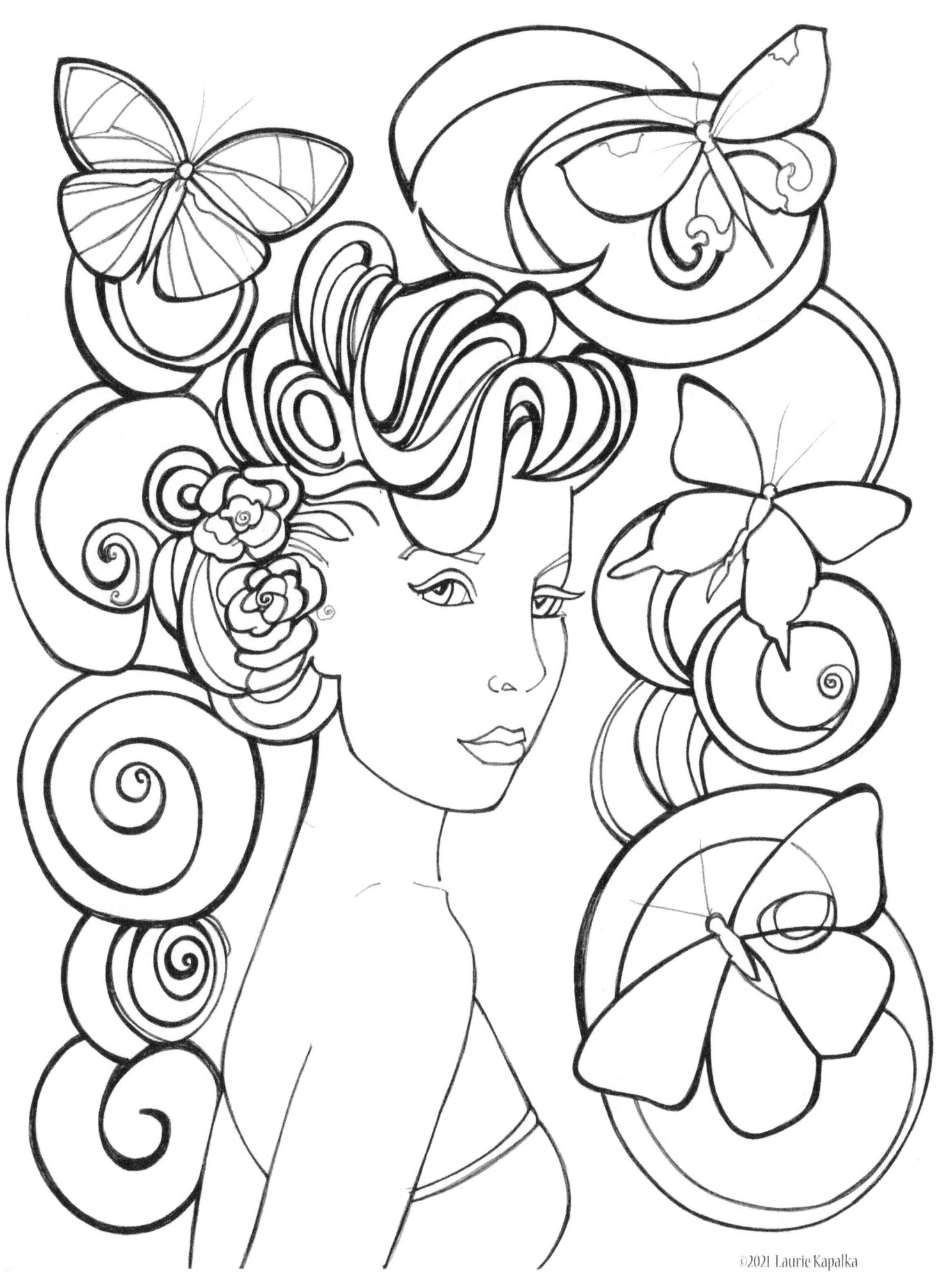

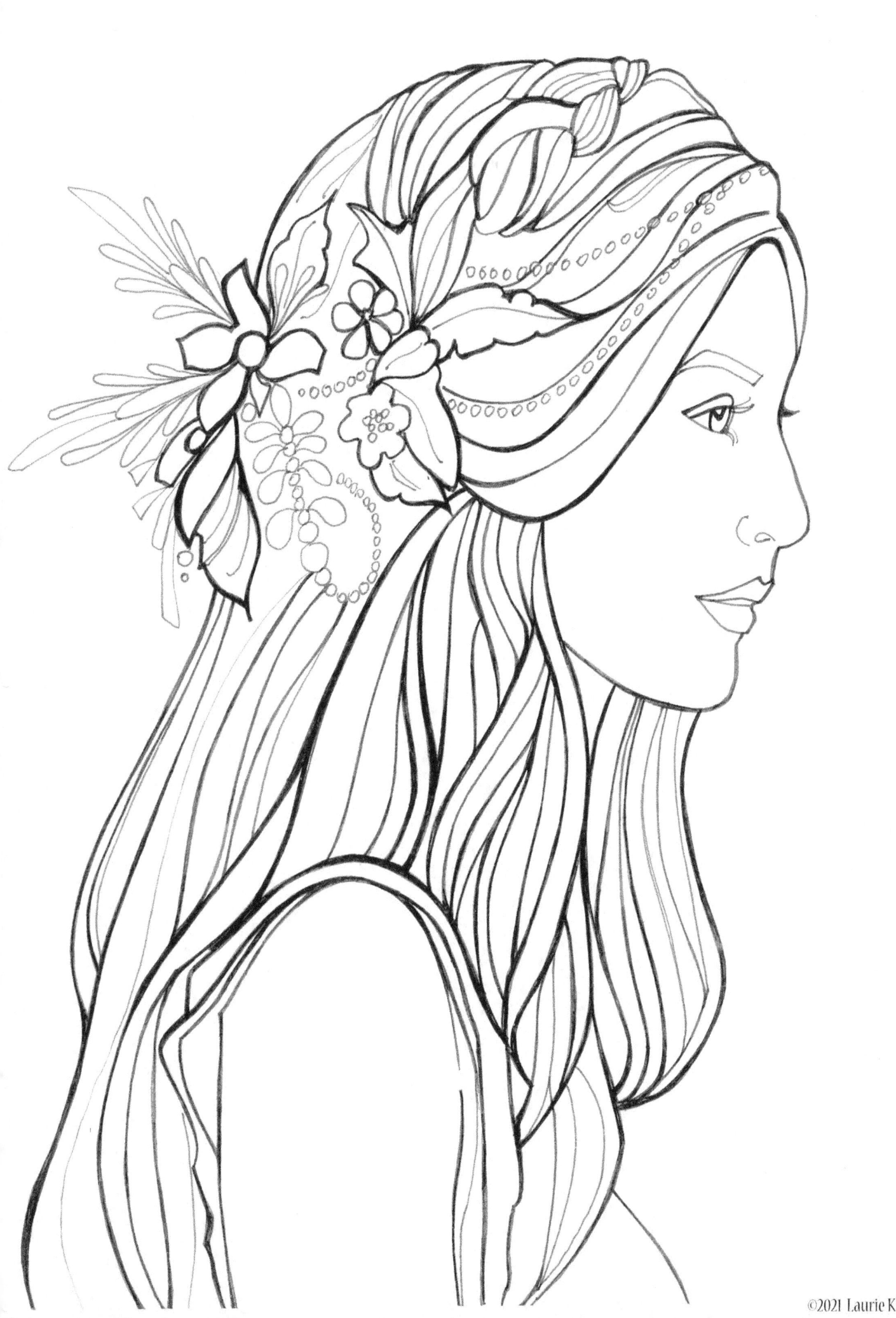

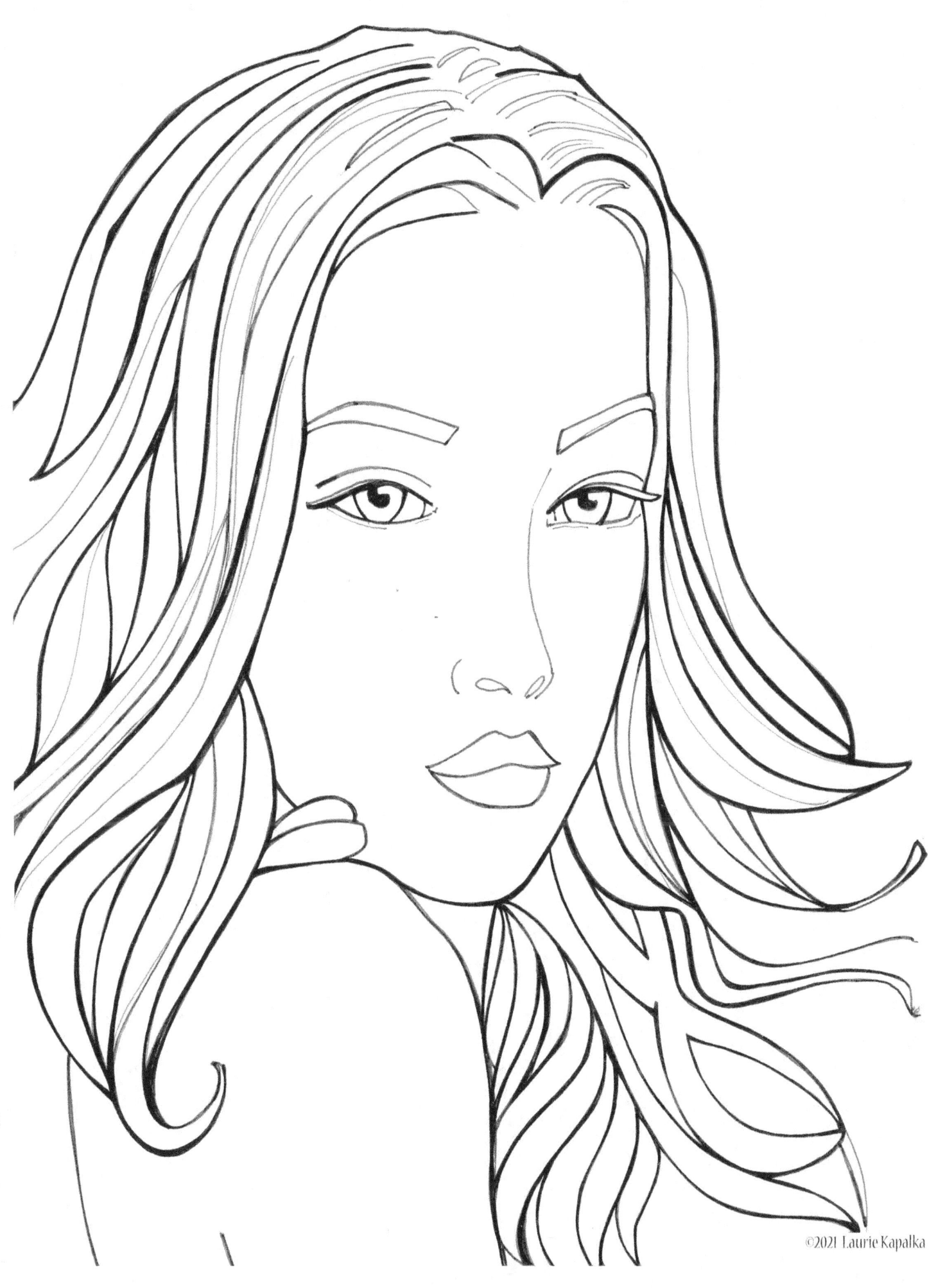

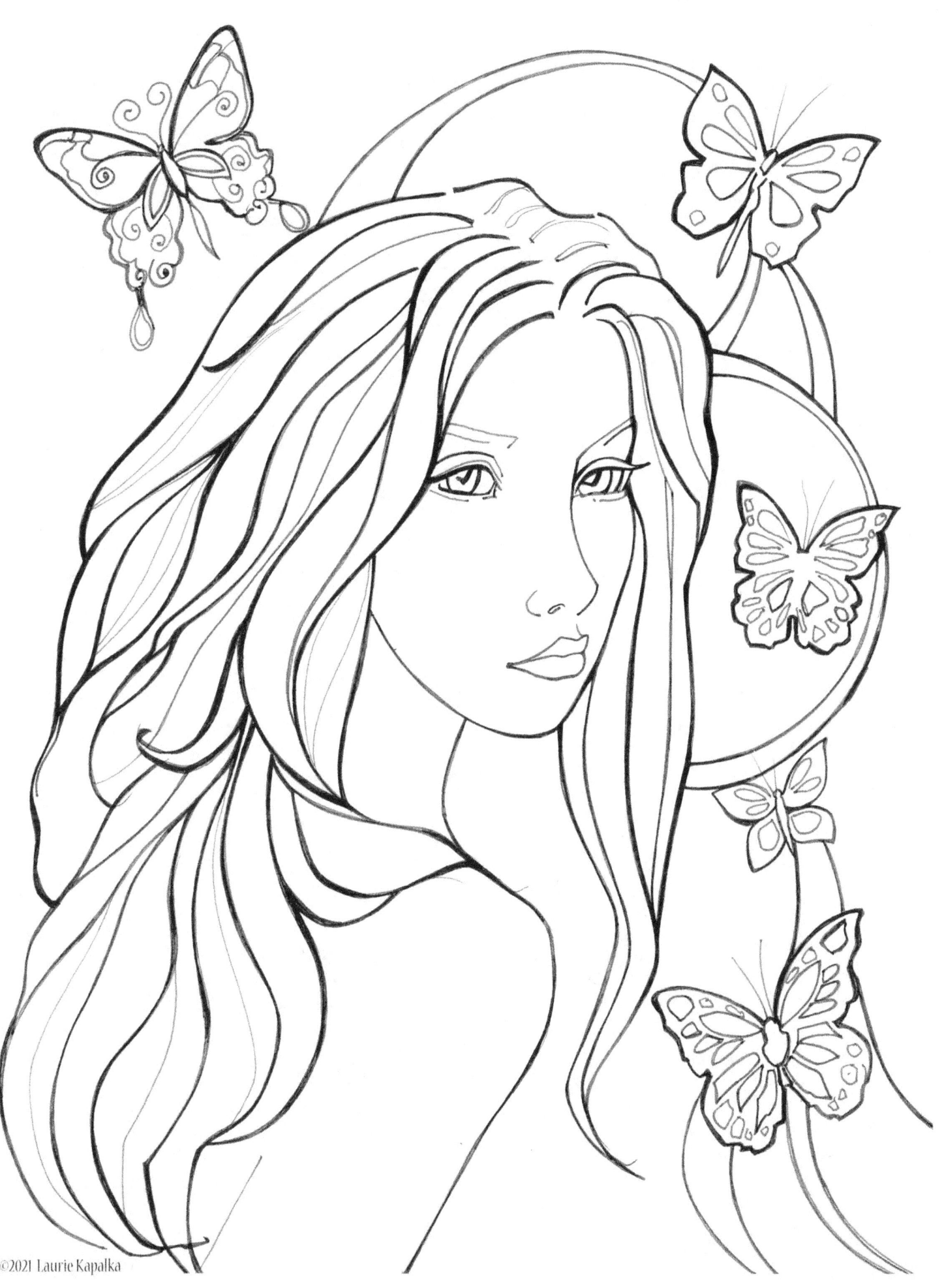

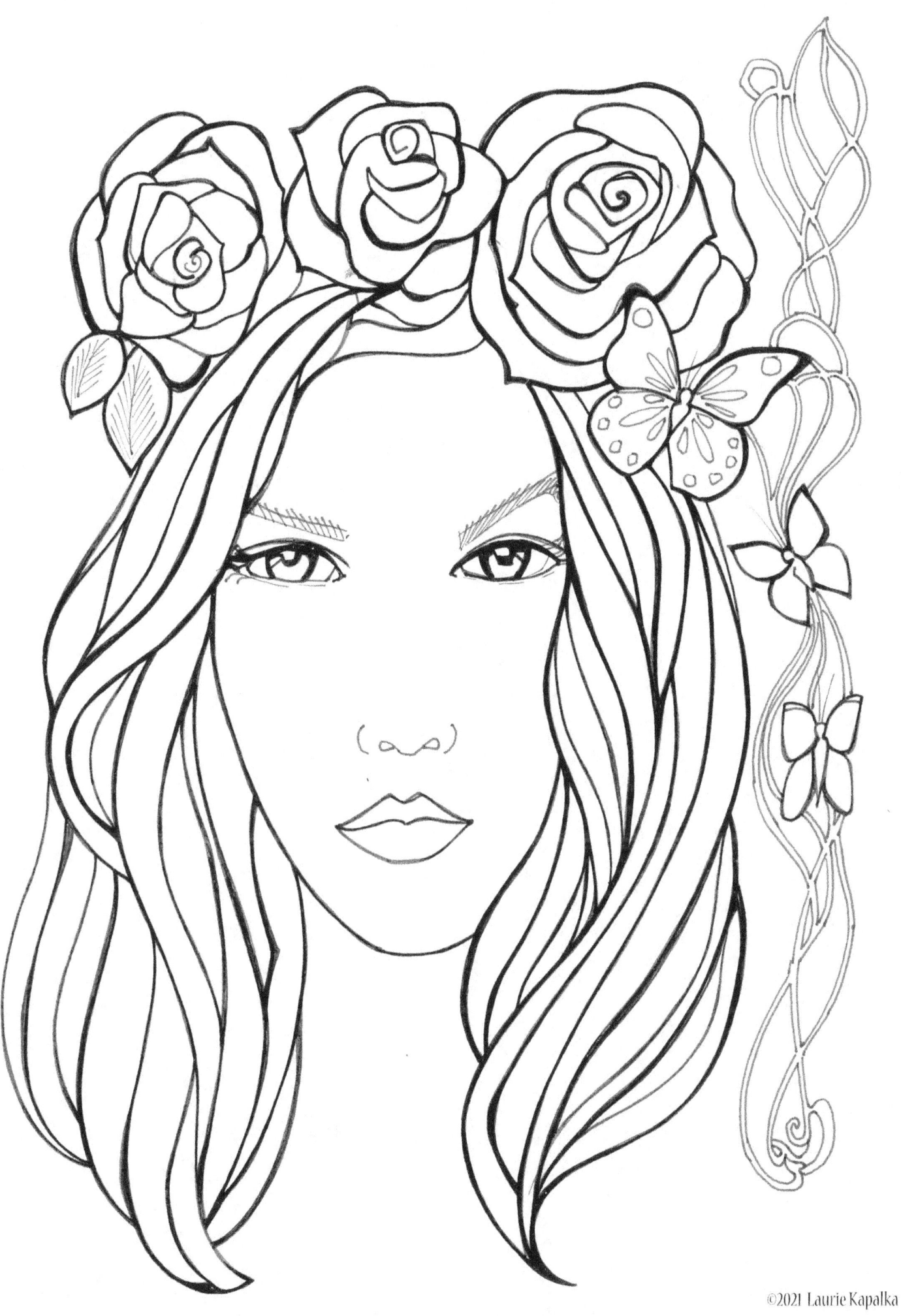
©2021 Laurie Kapalka

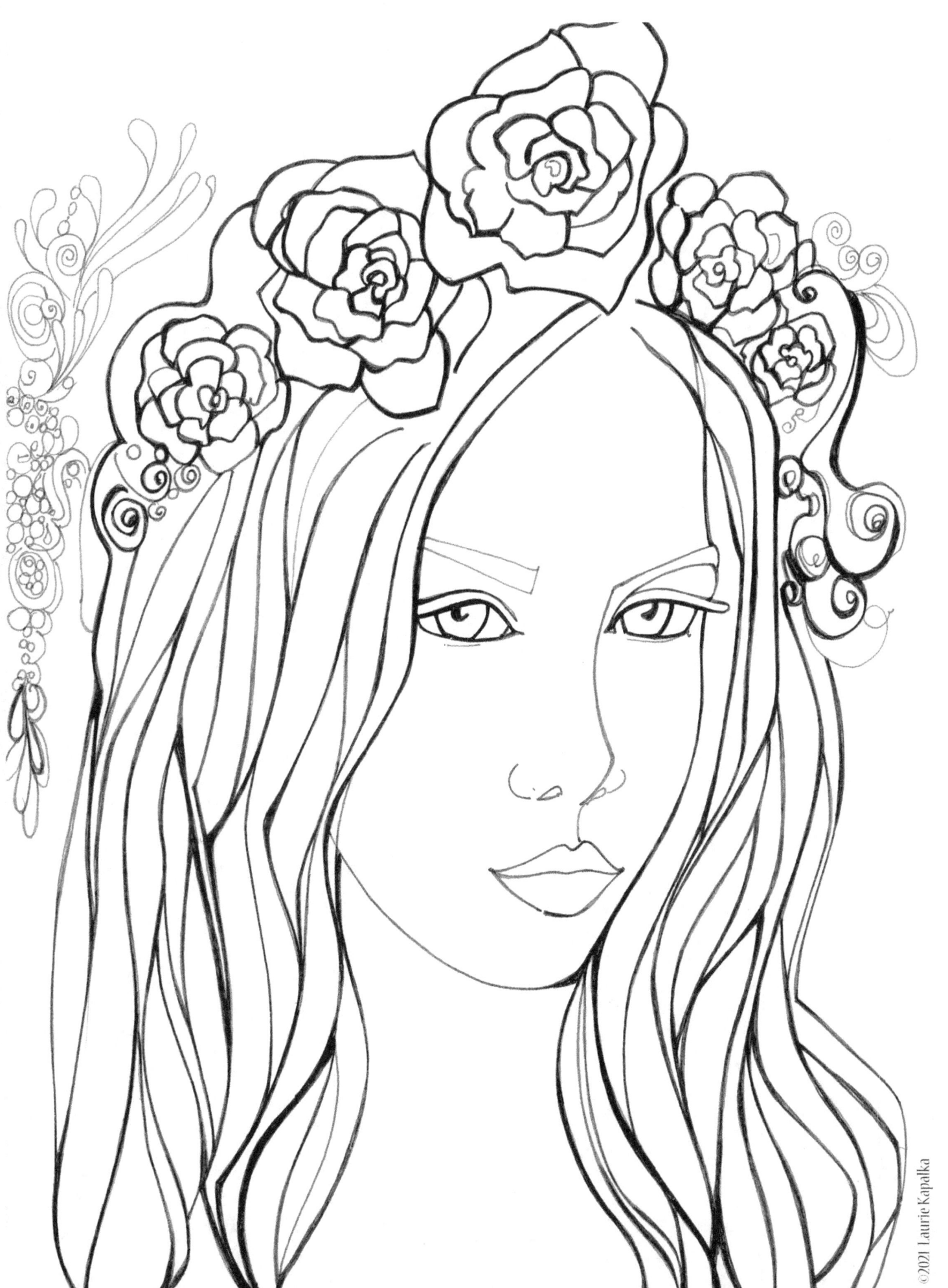

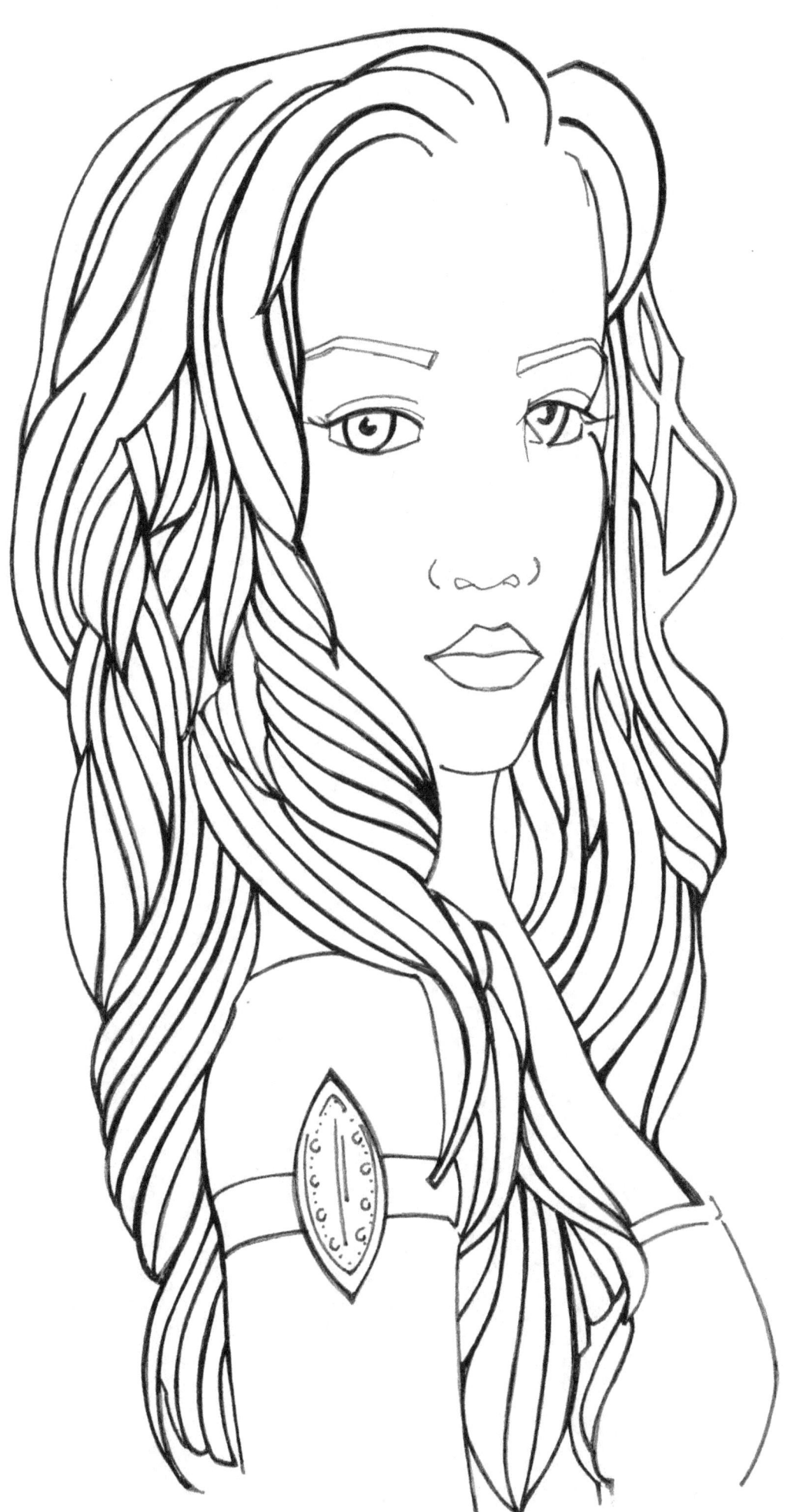

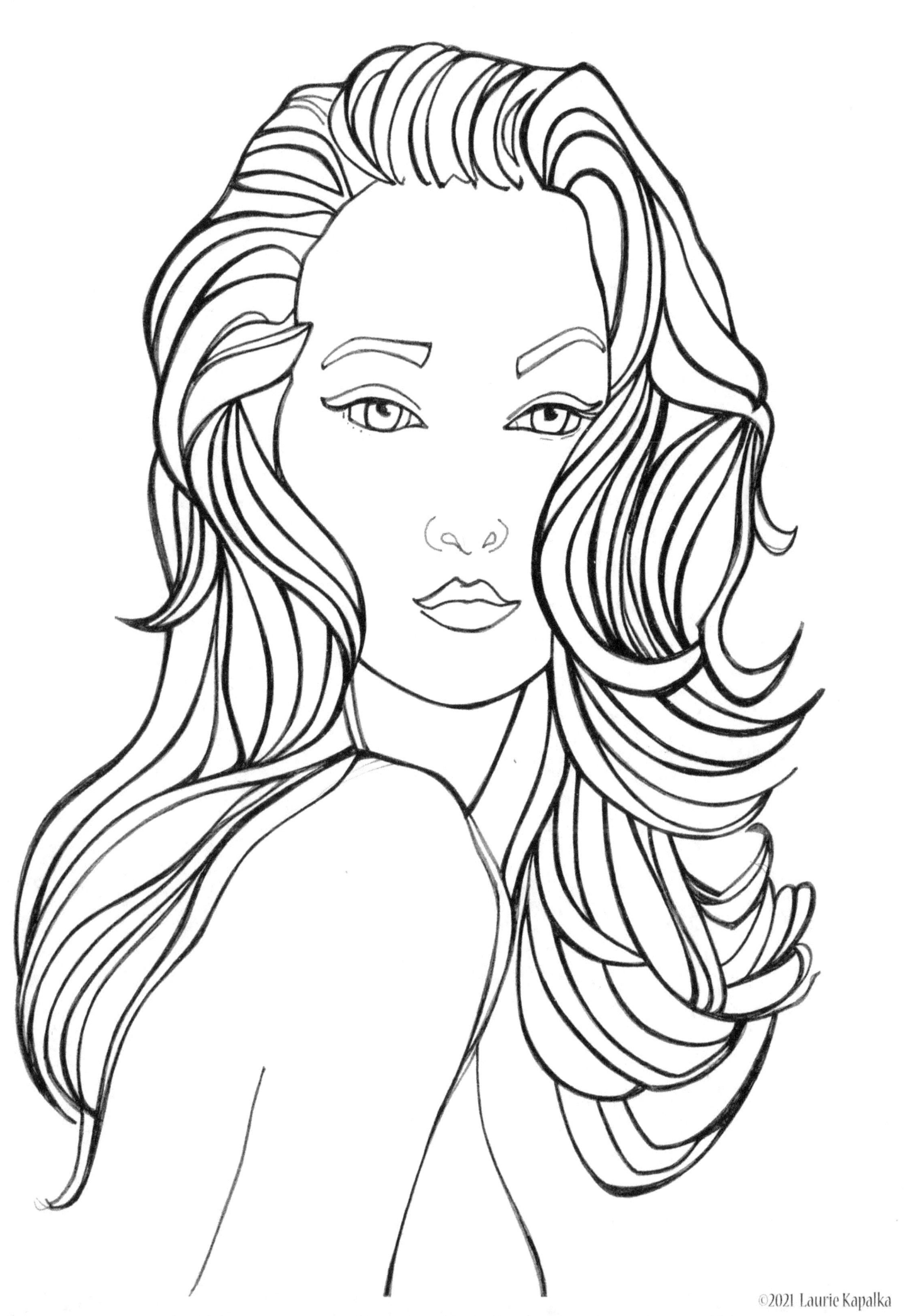

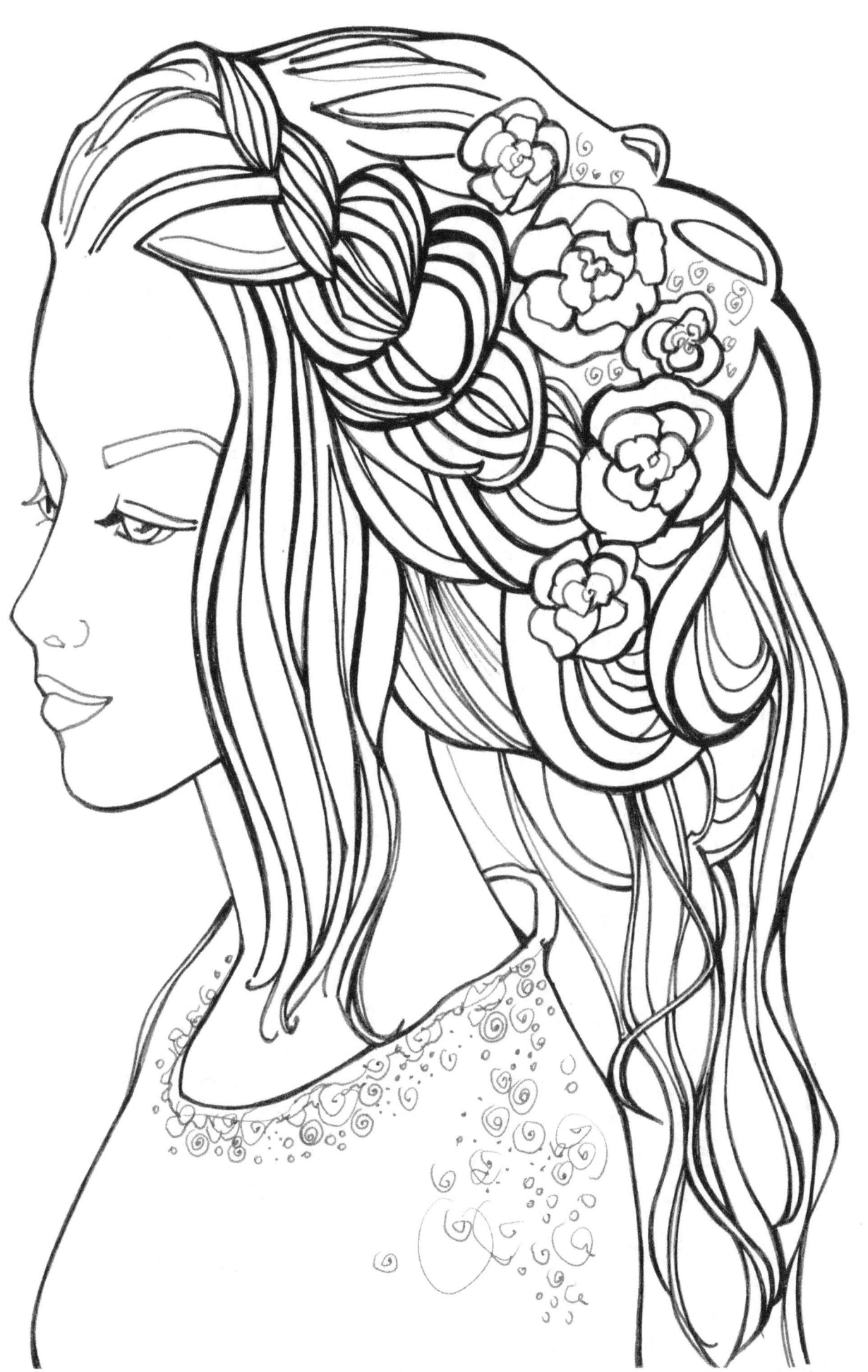

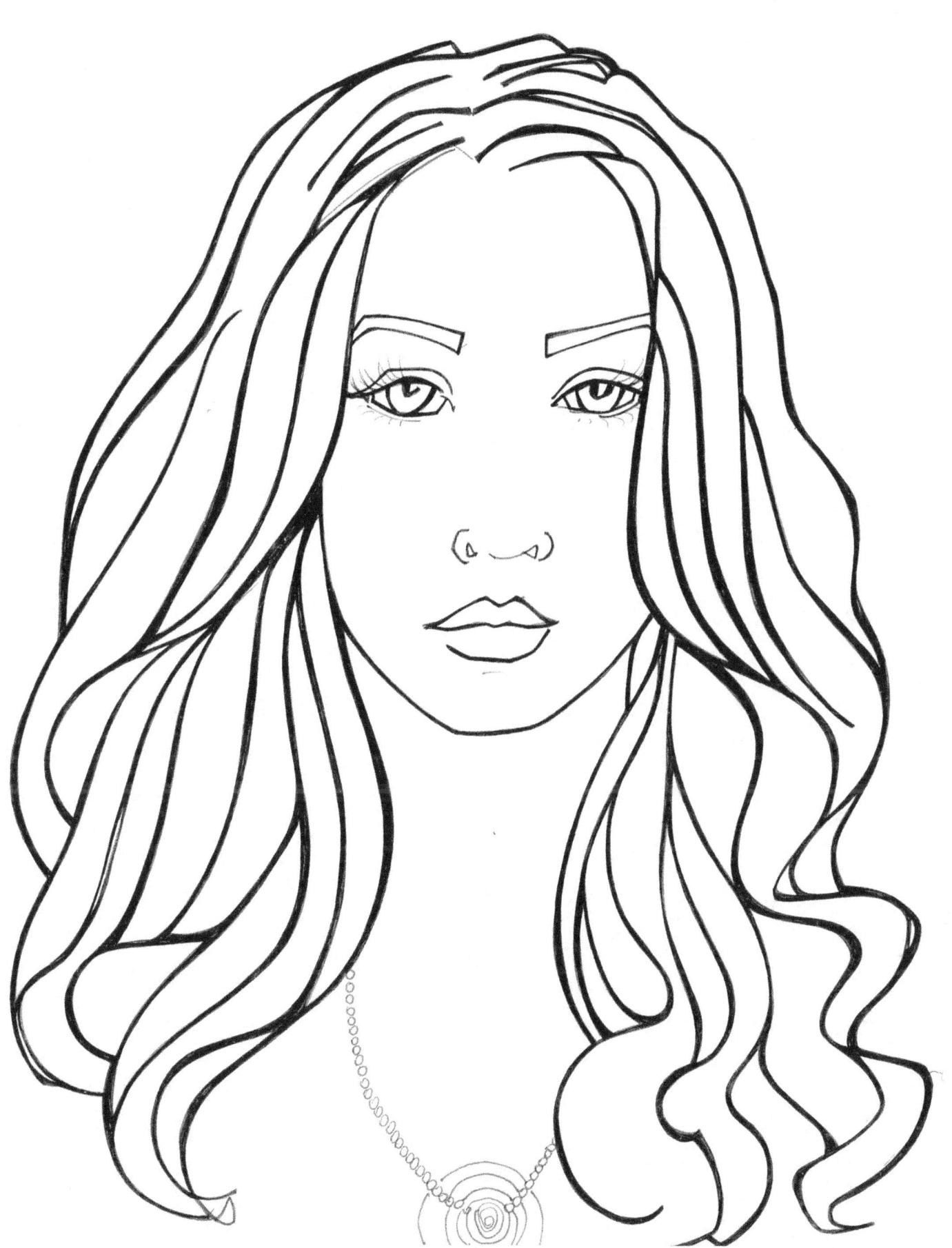

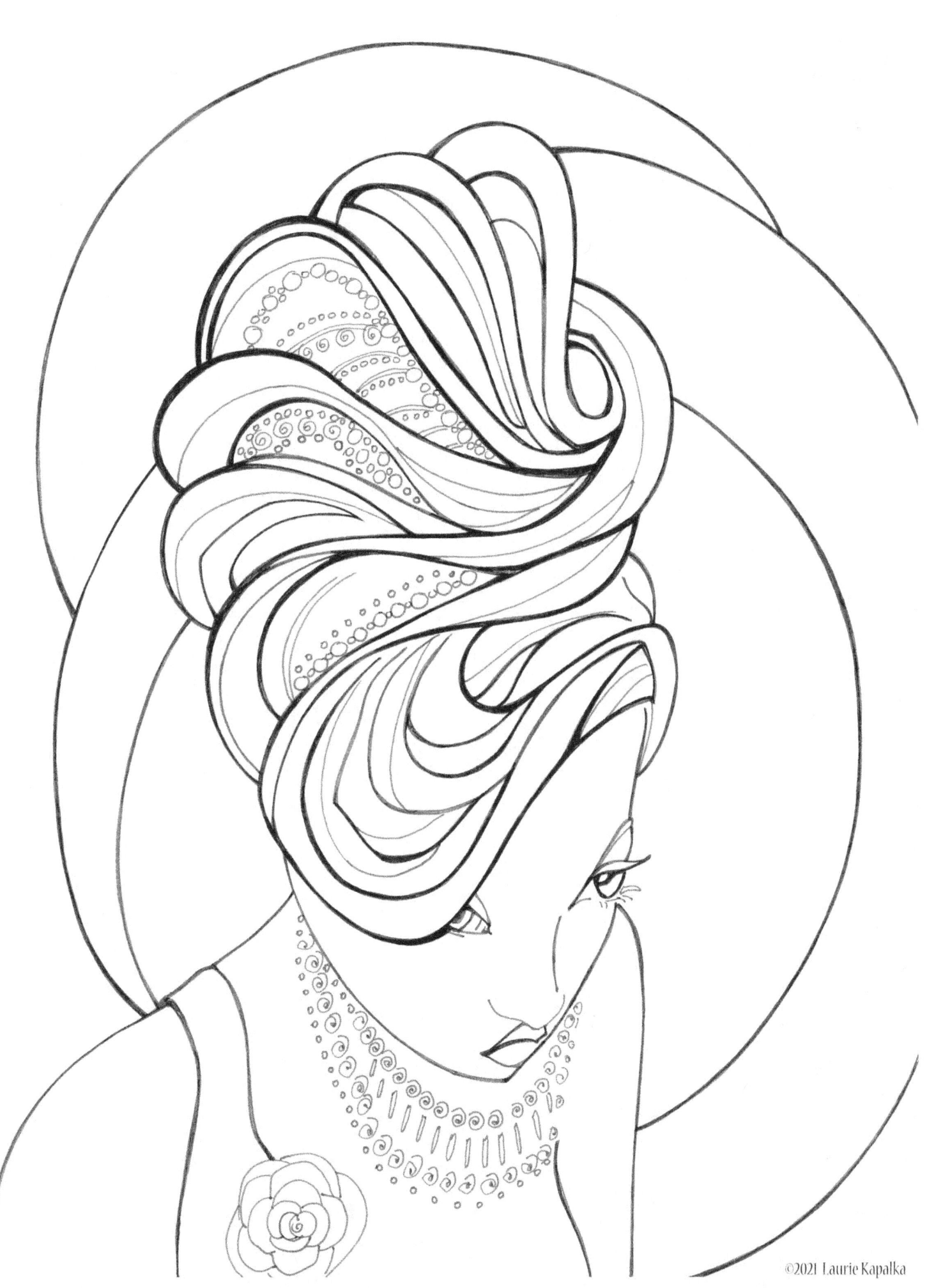

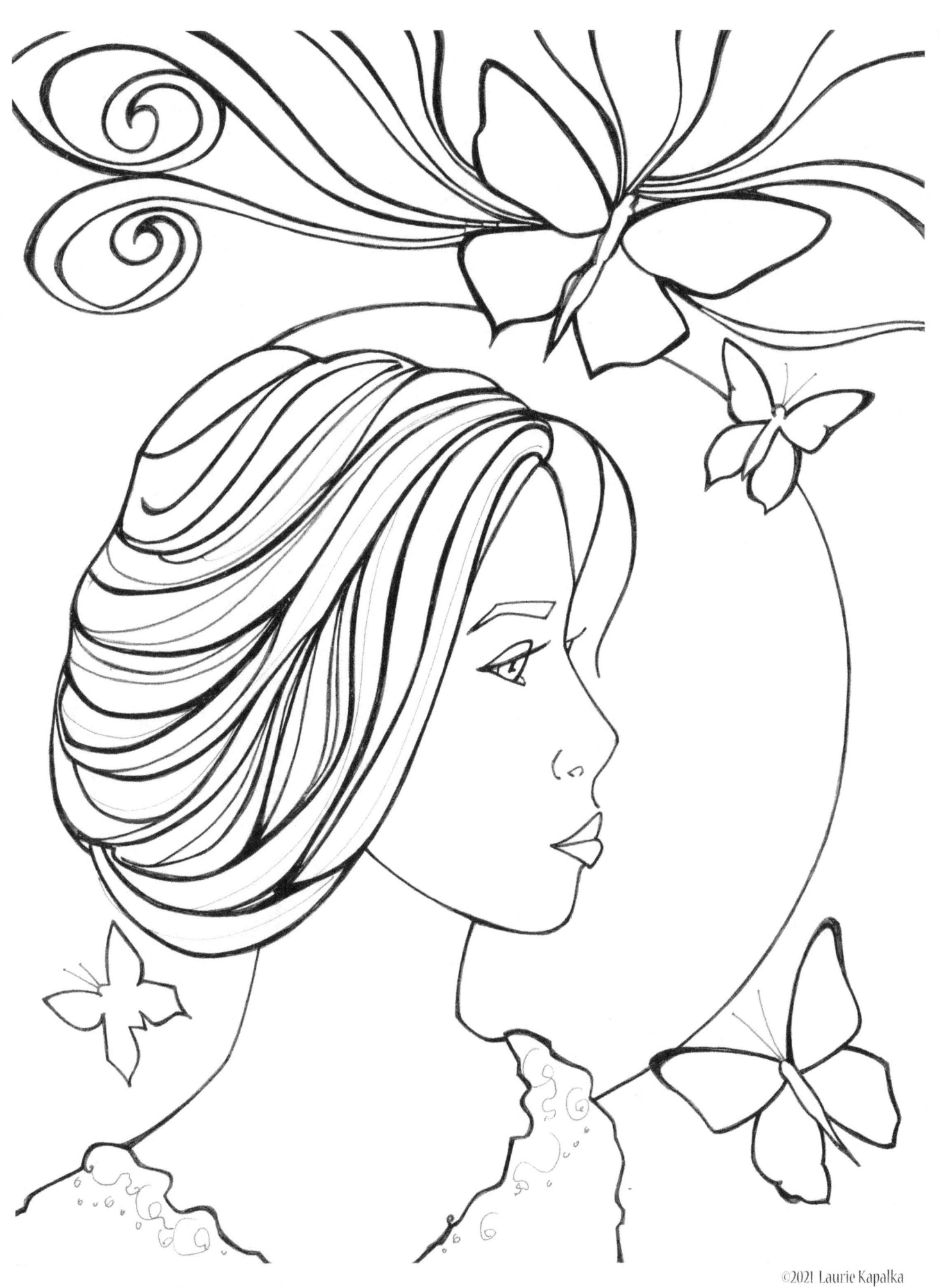

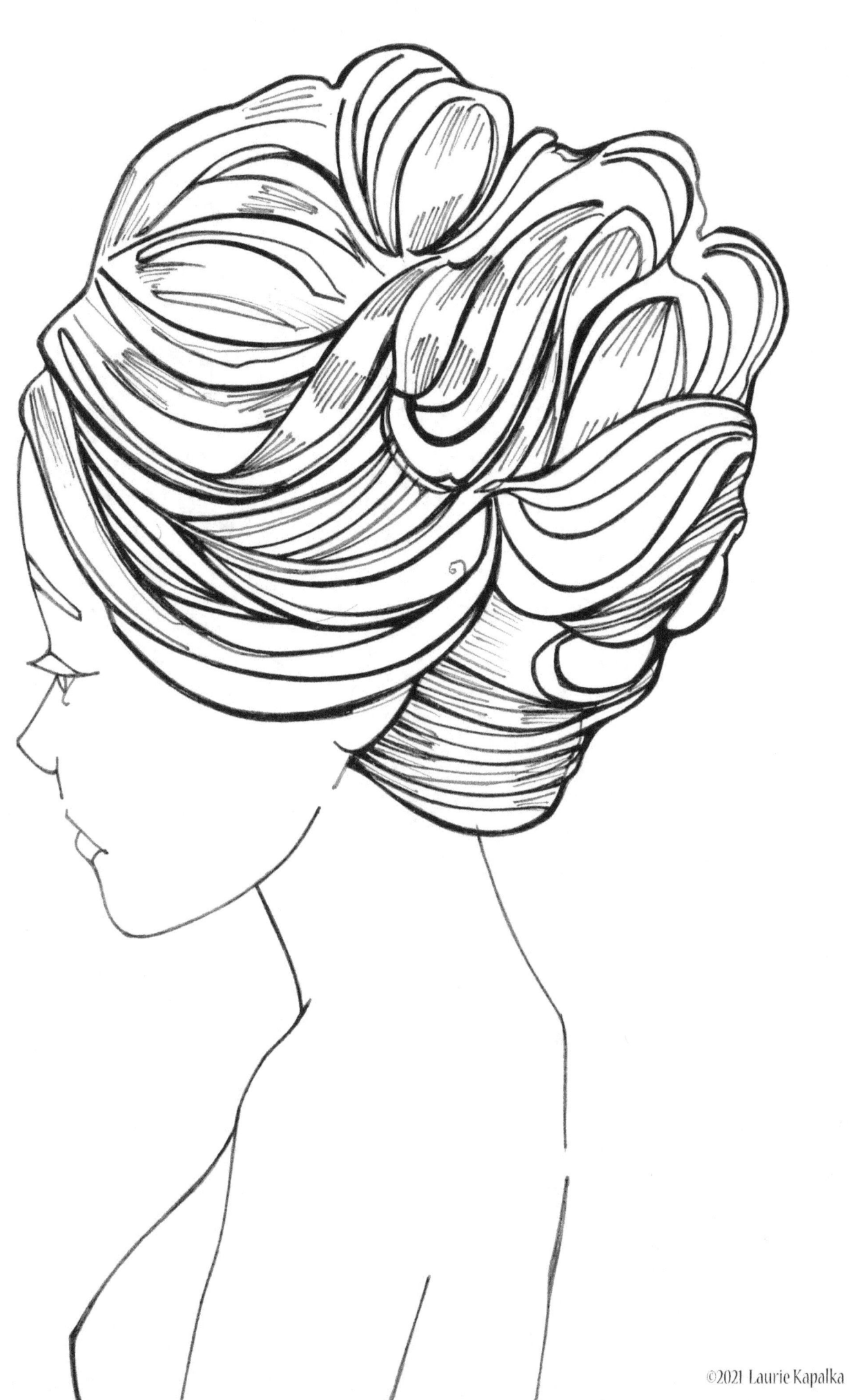

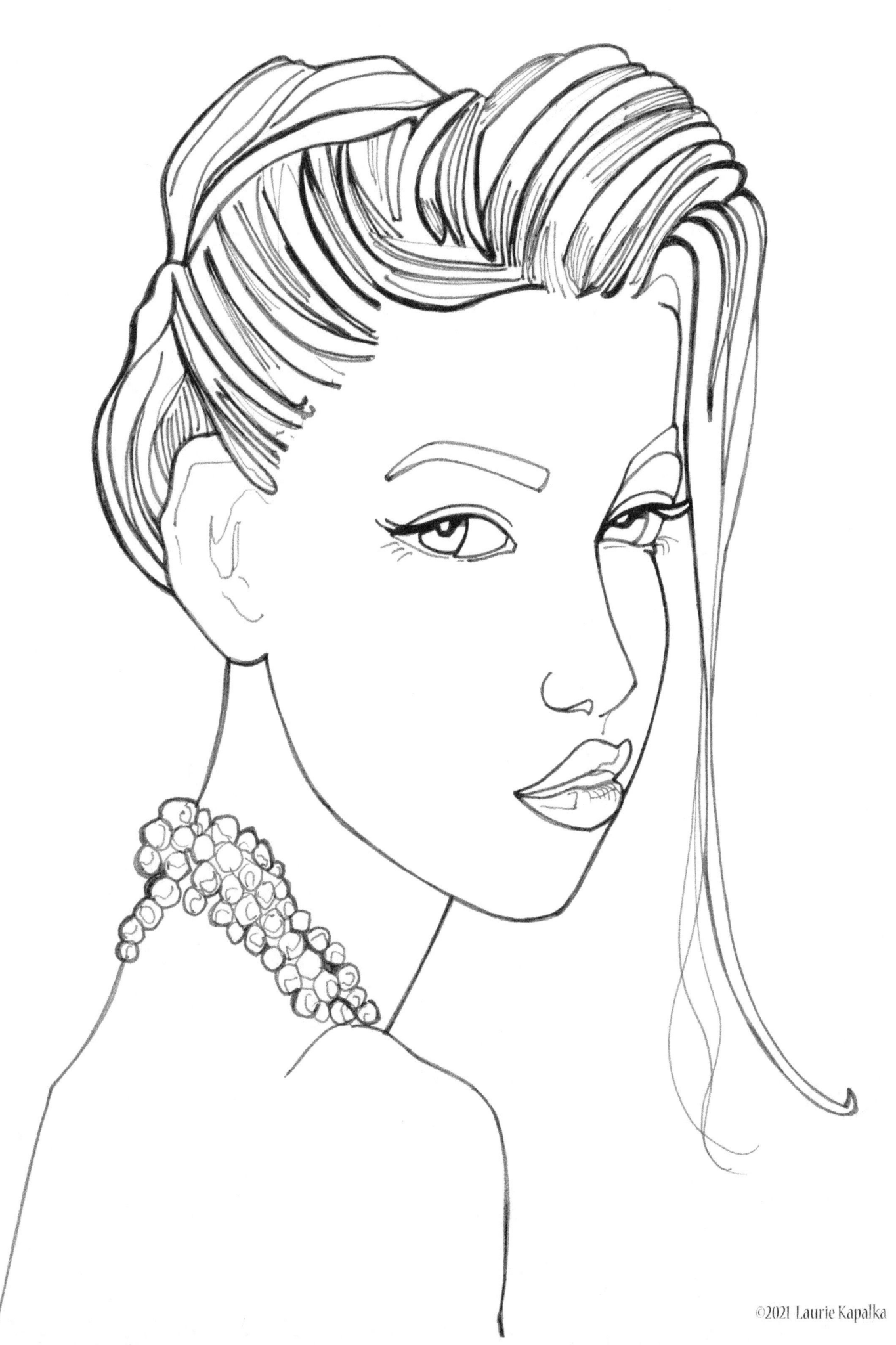

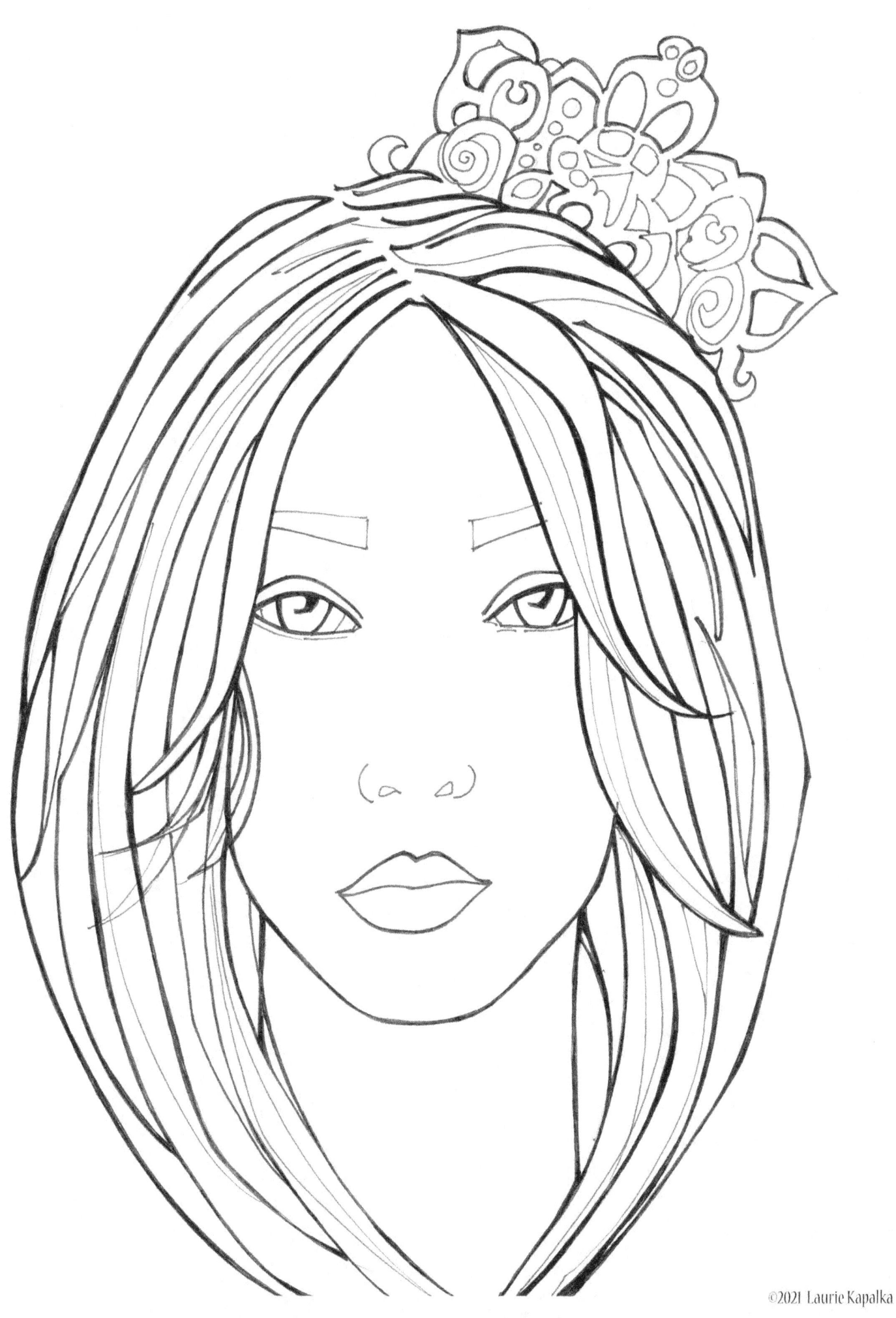

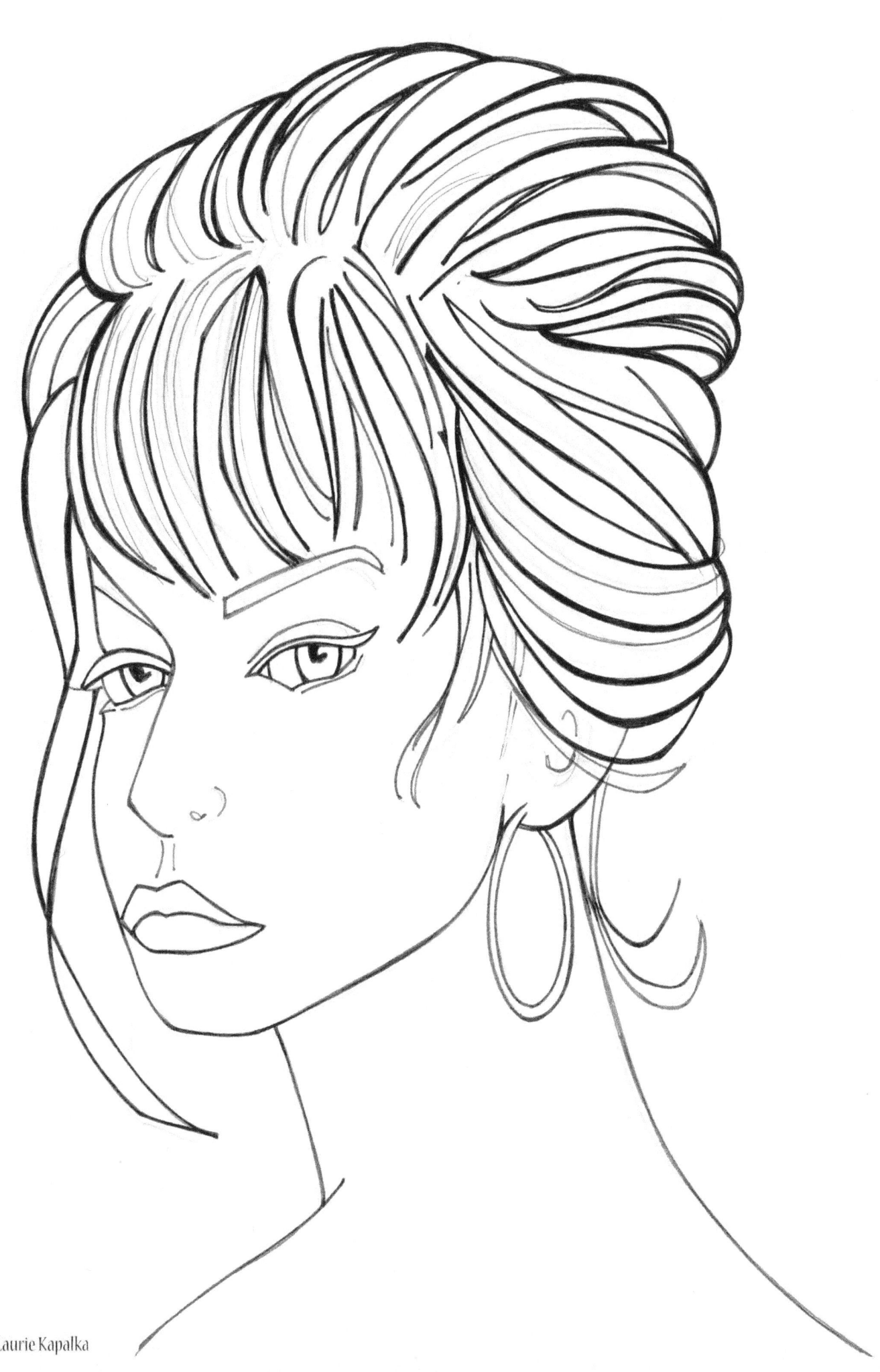

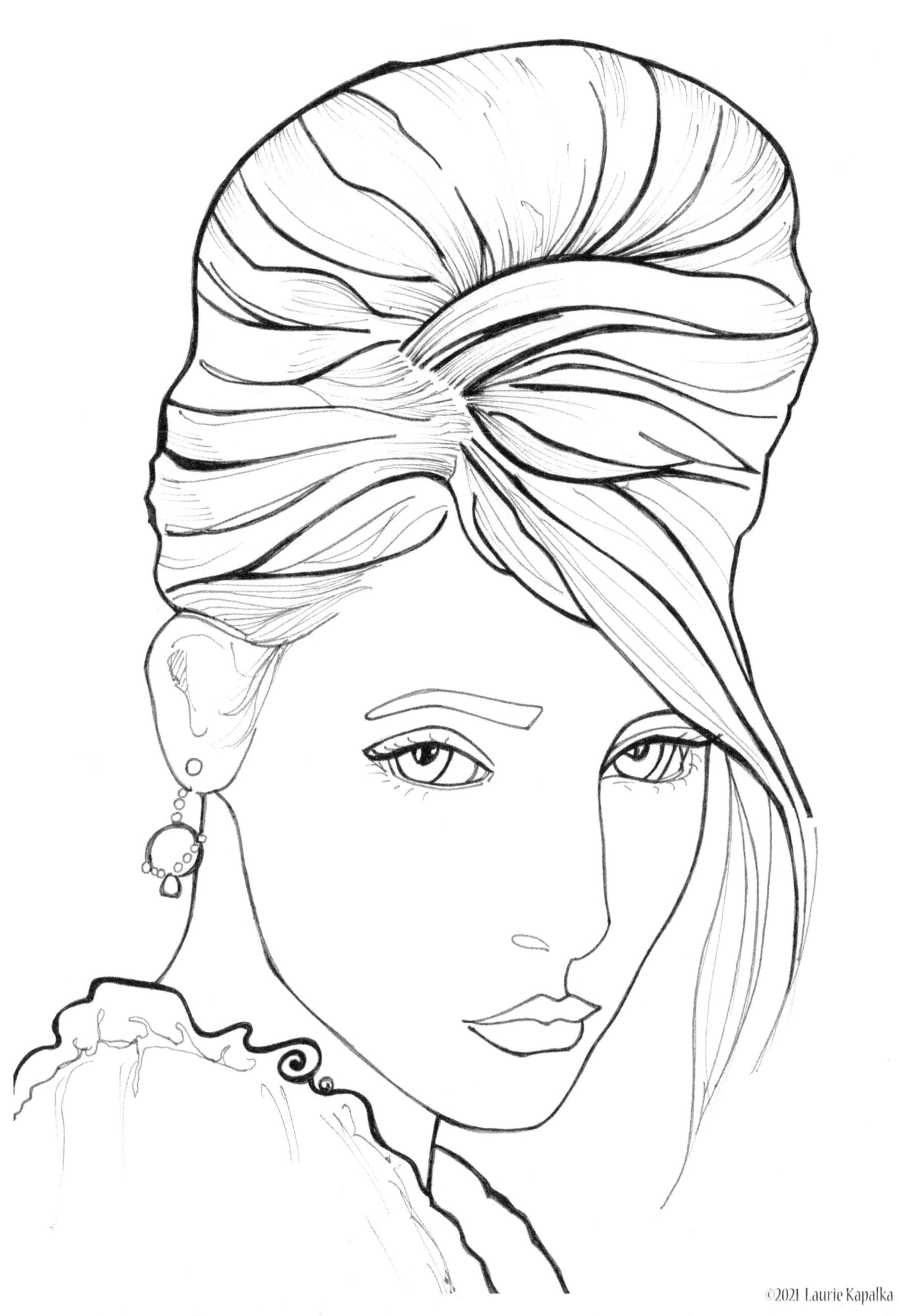

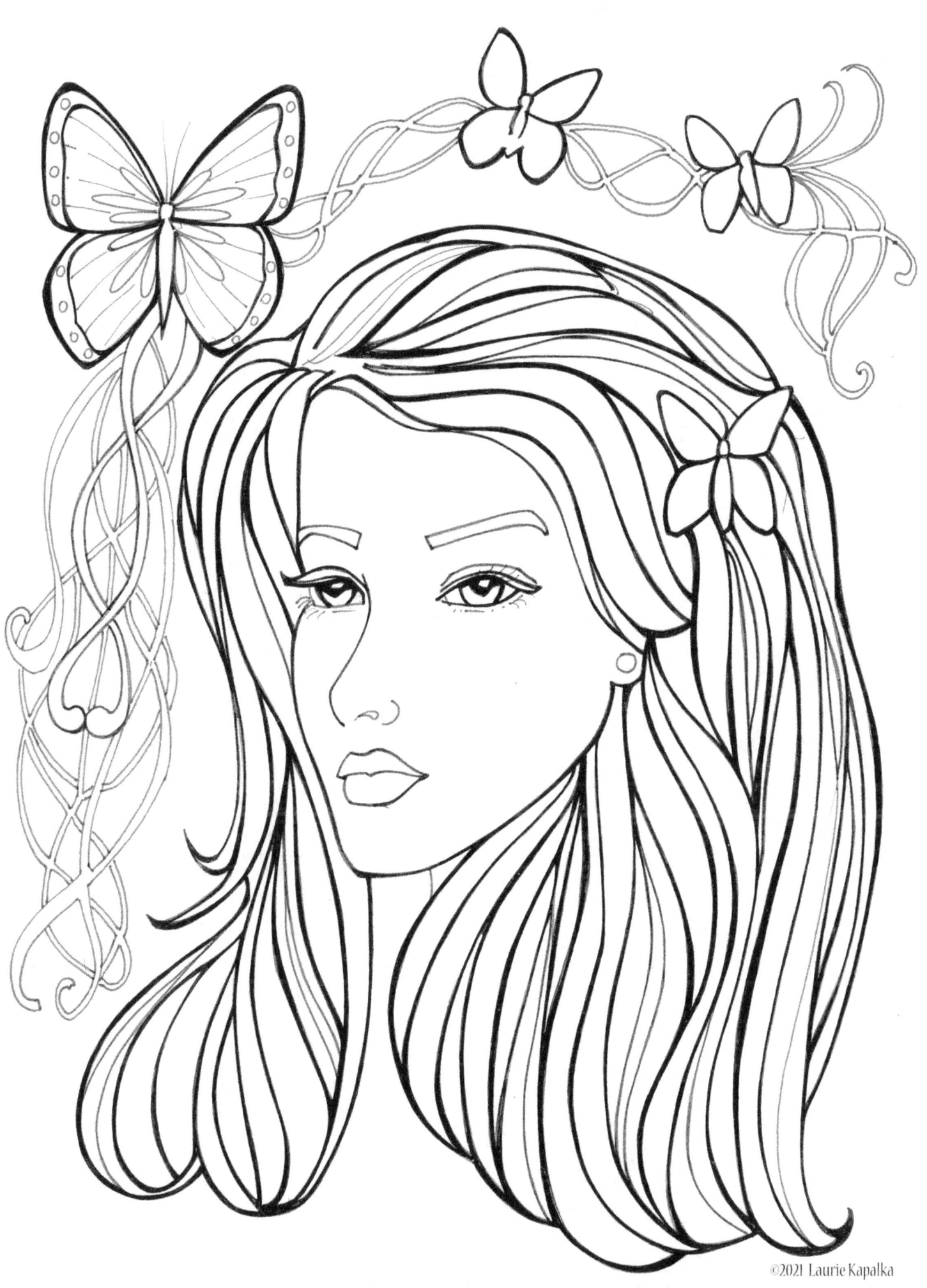

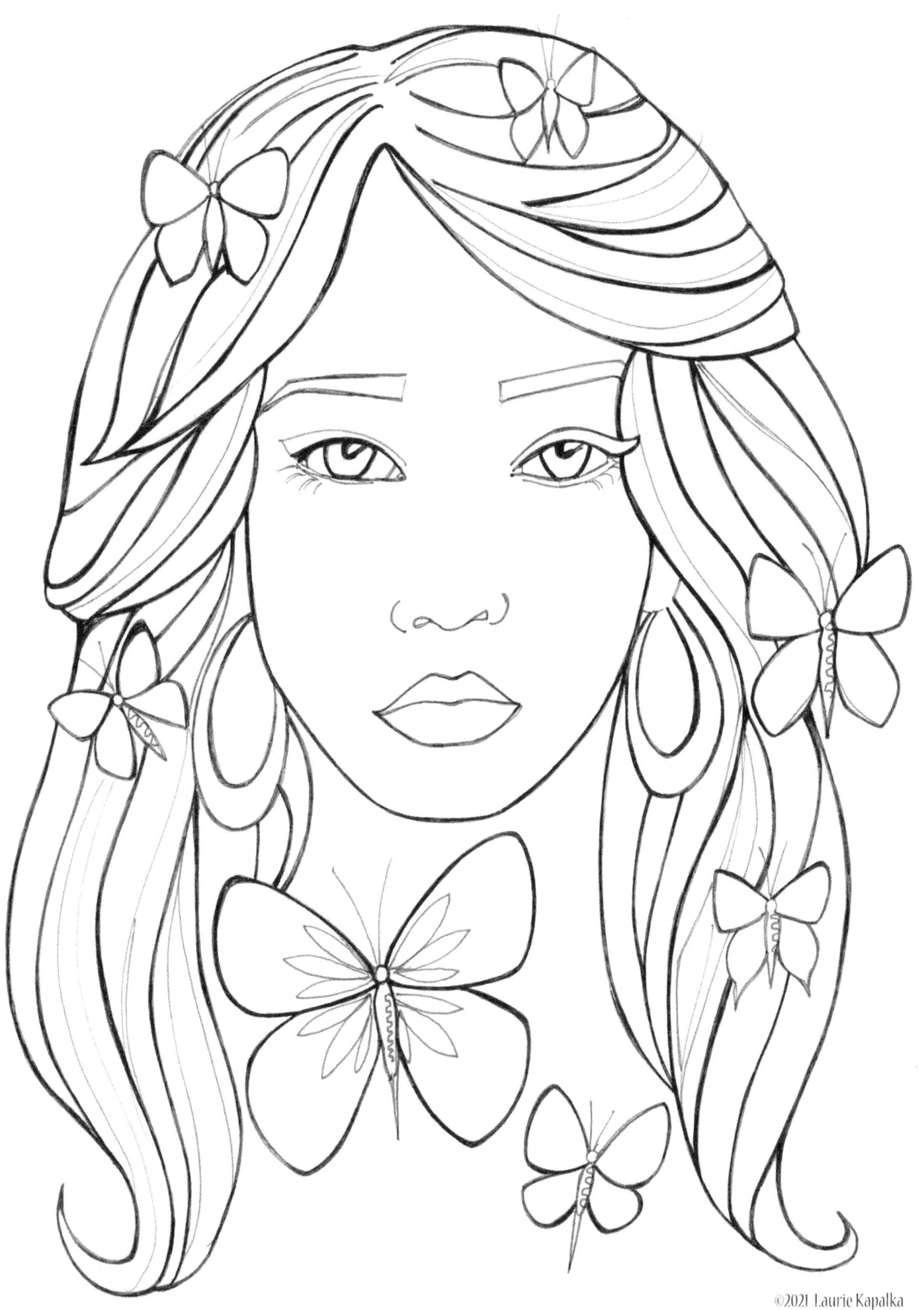

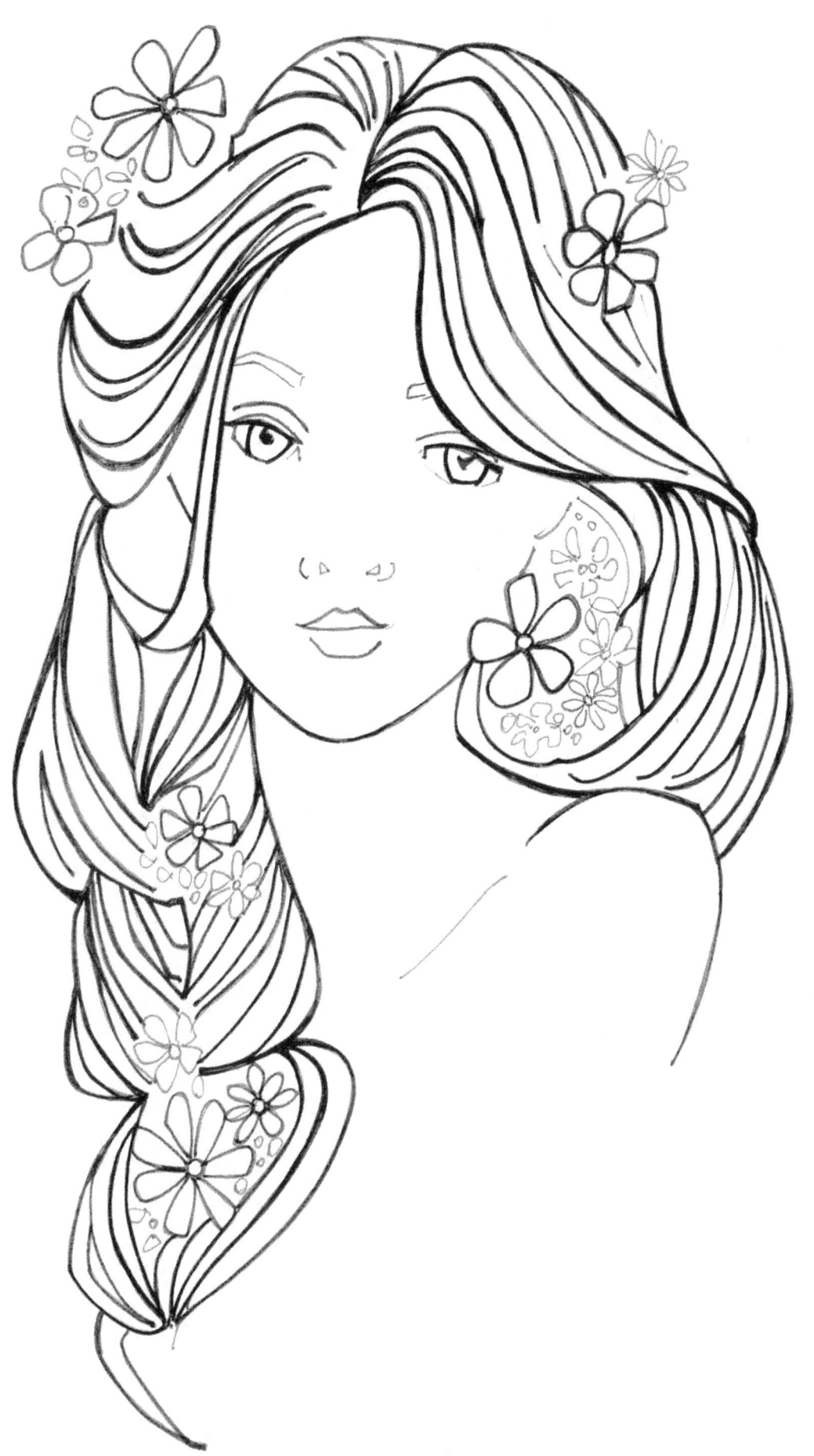

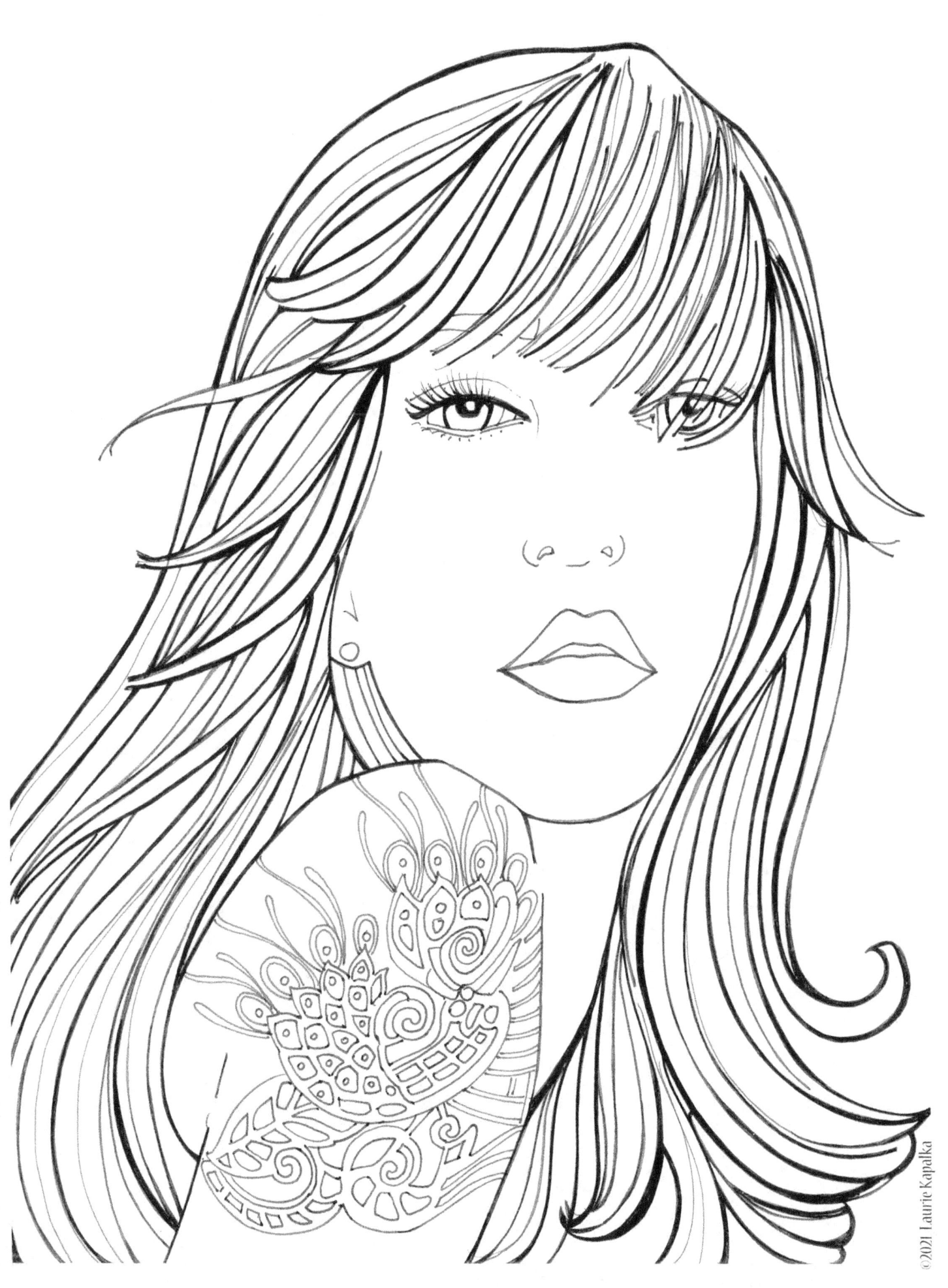

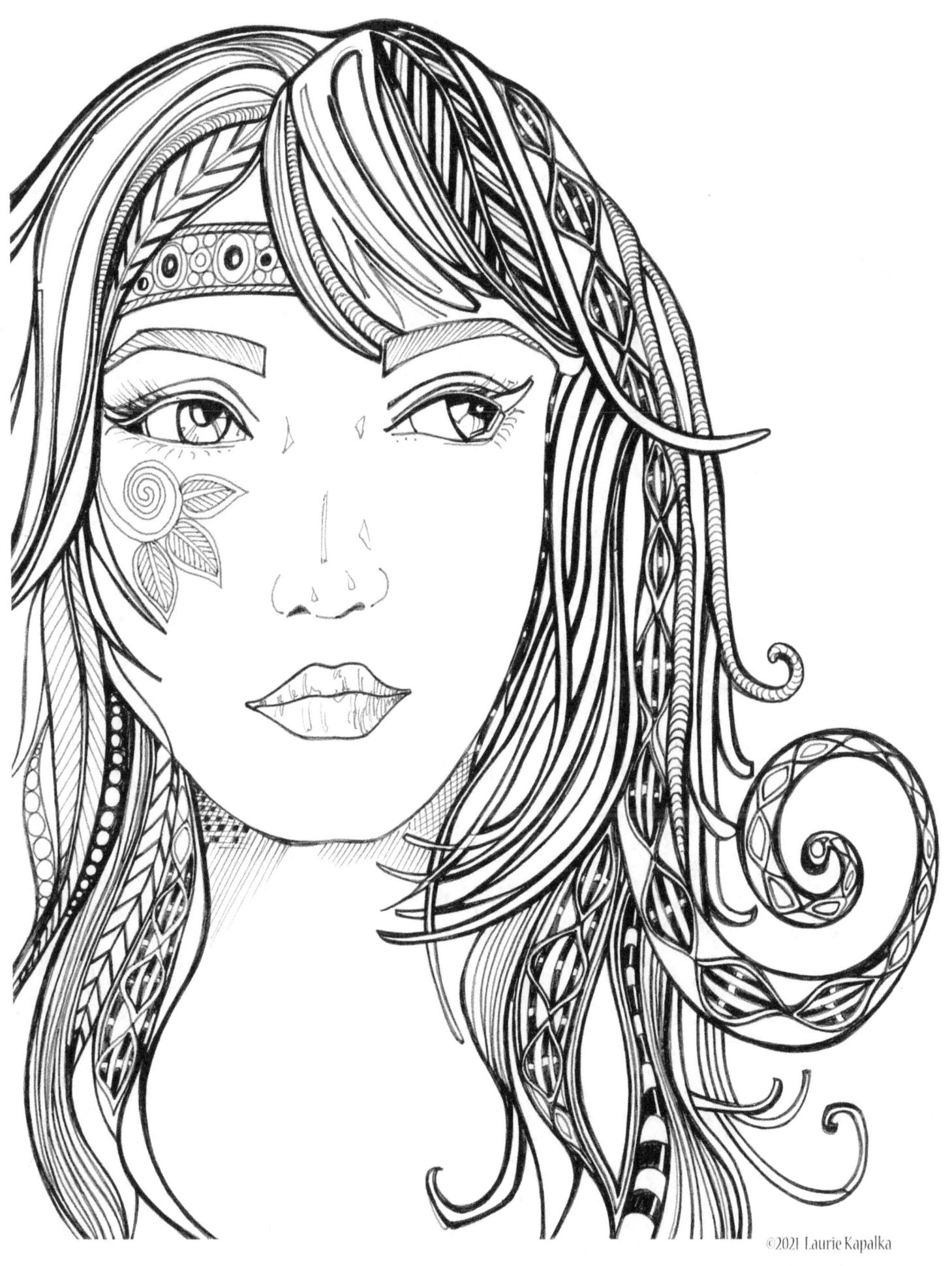

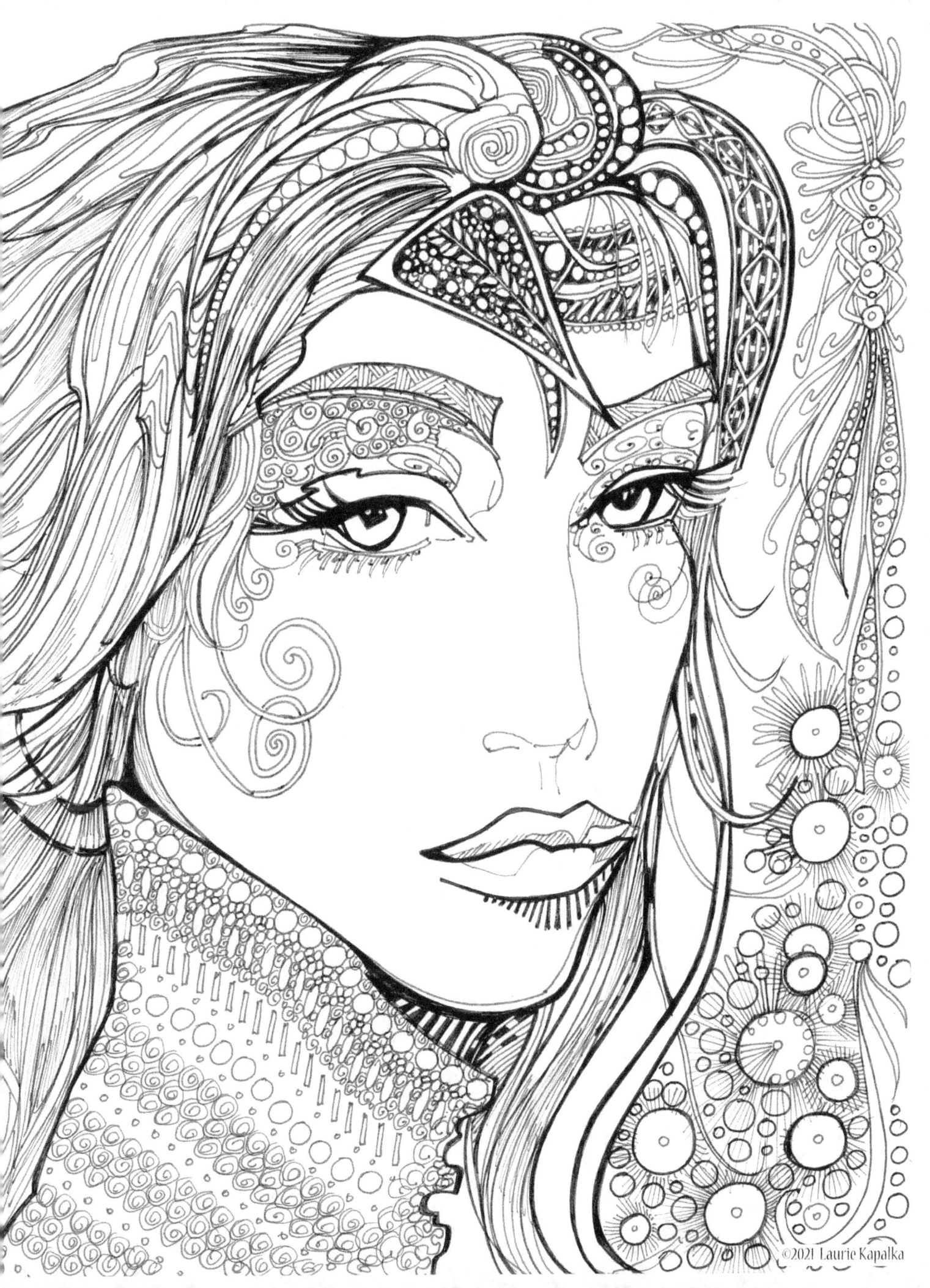

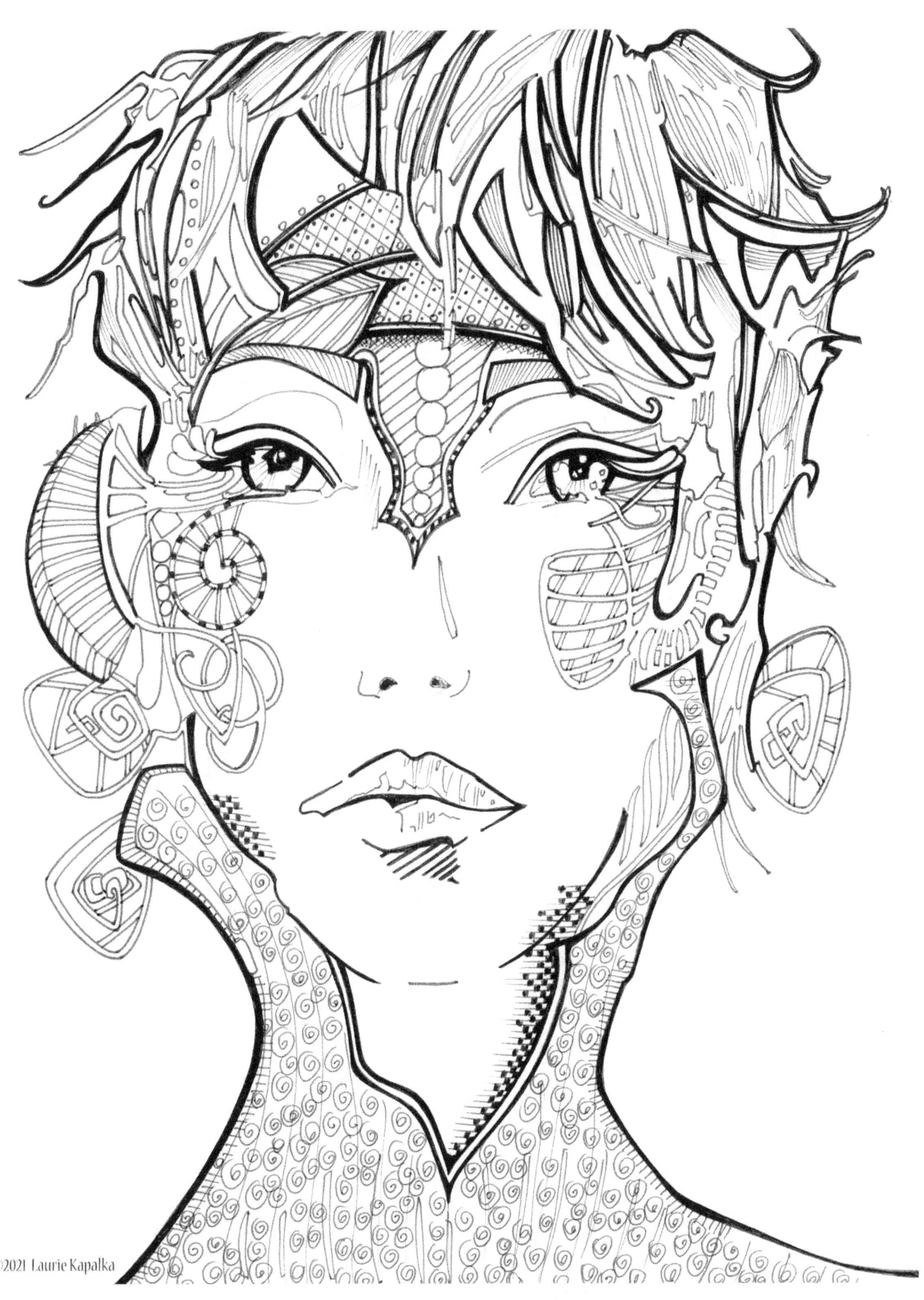

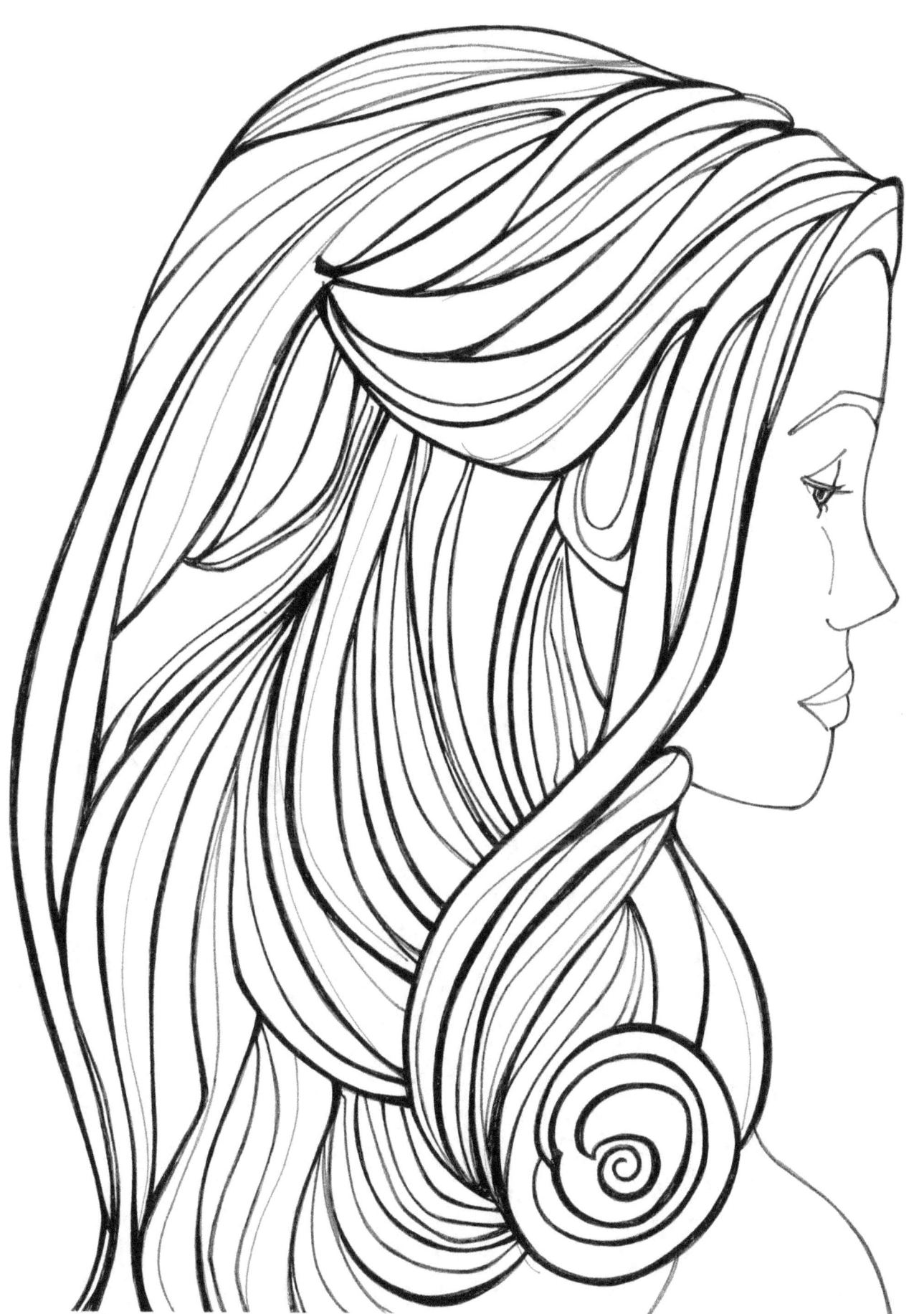

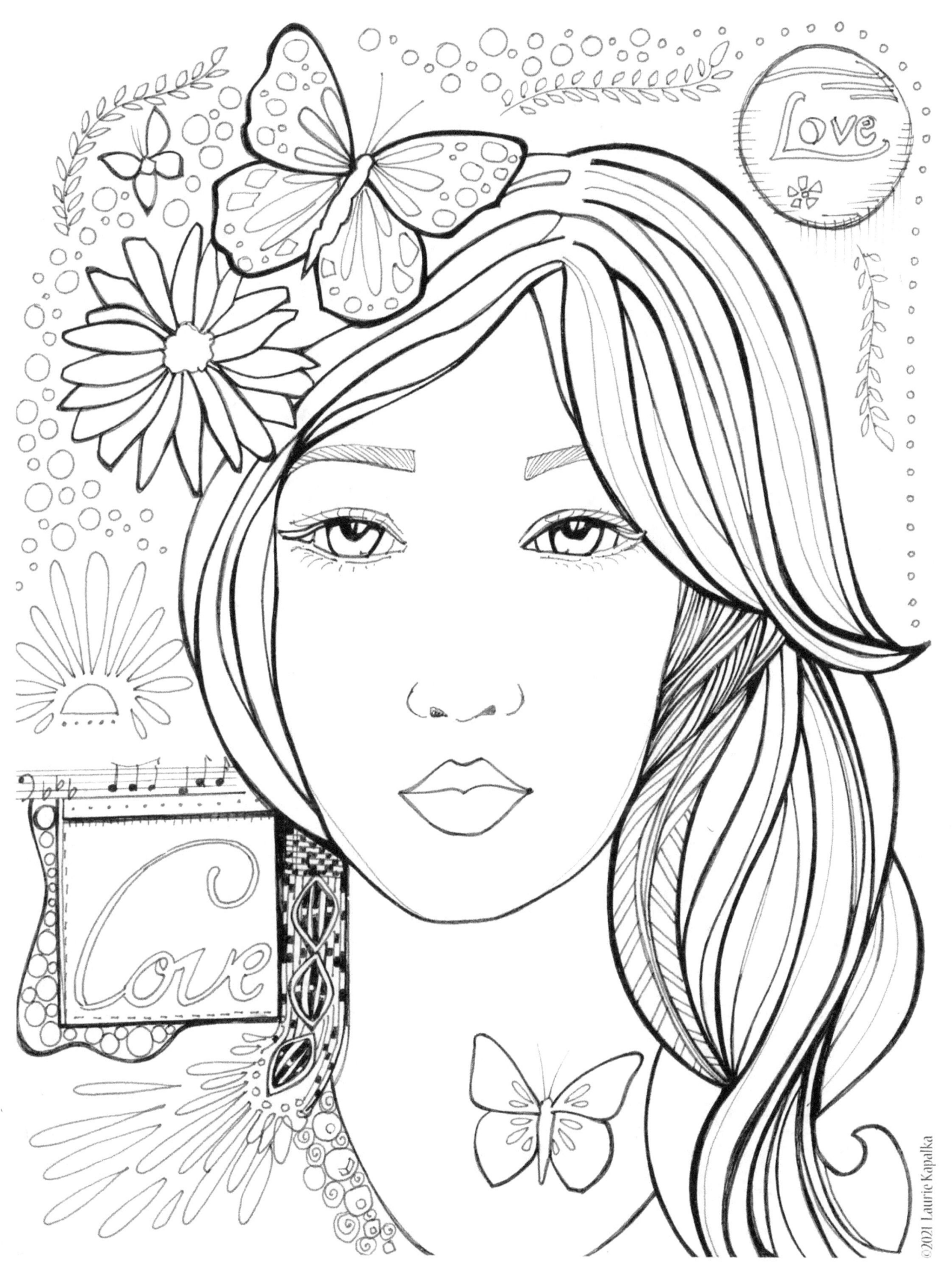

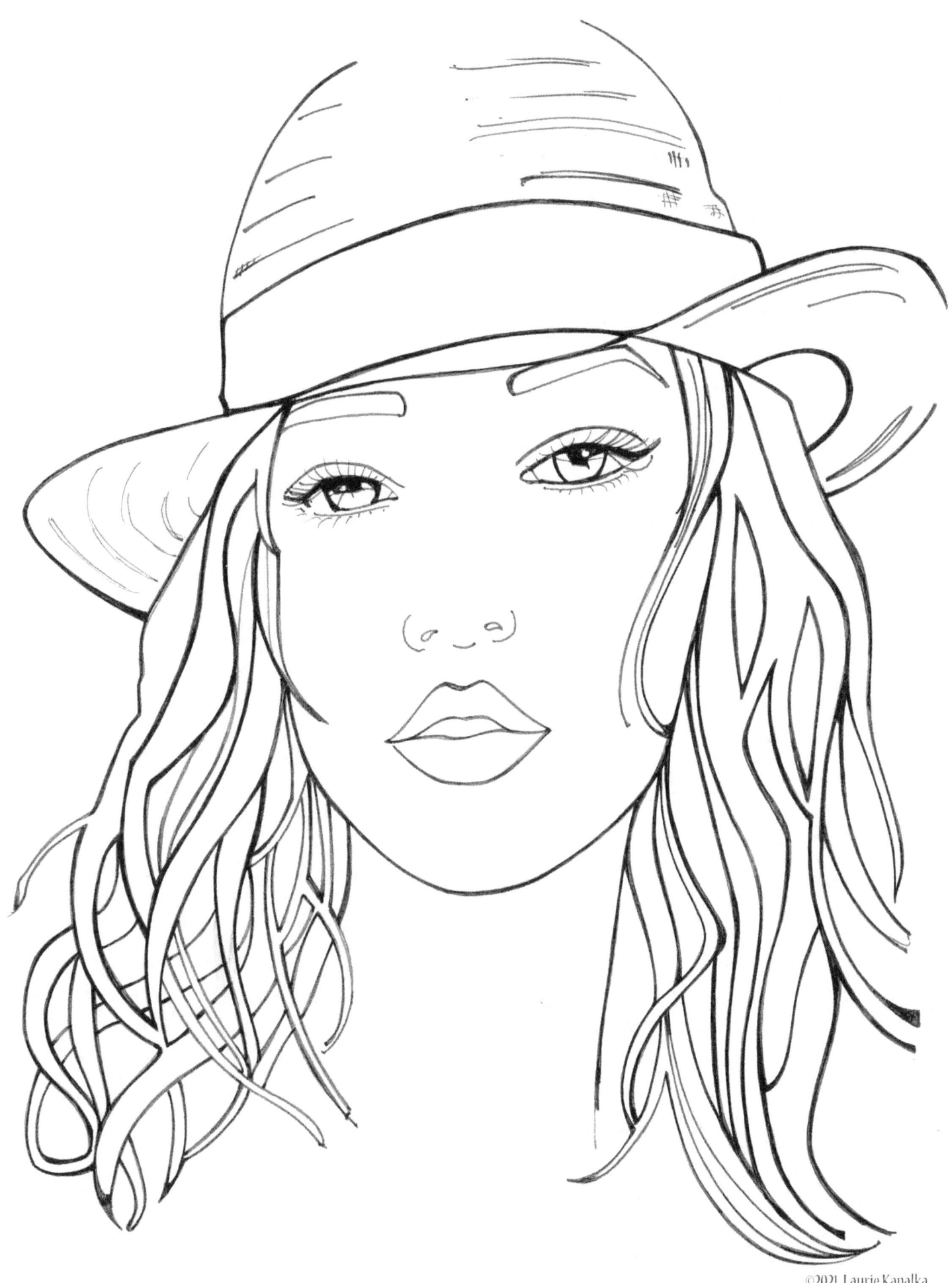

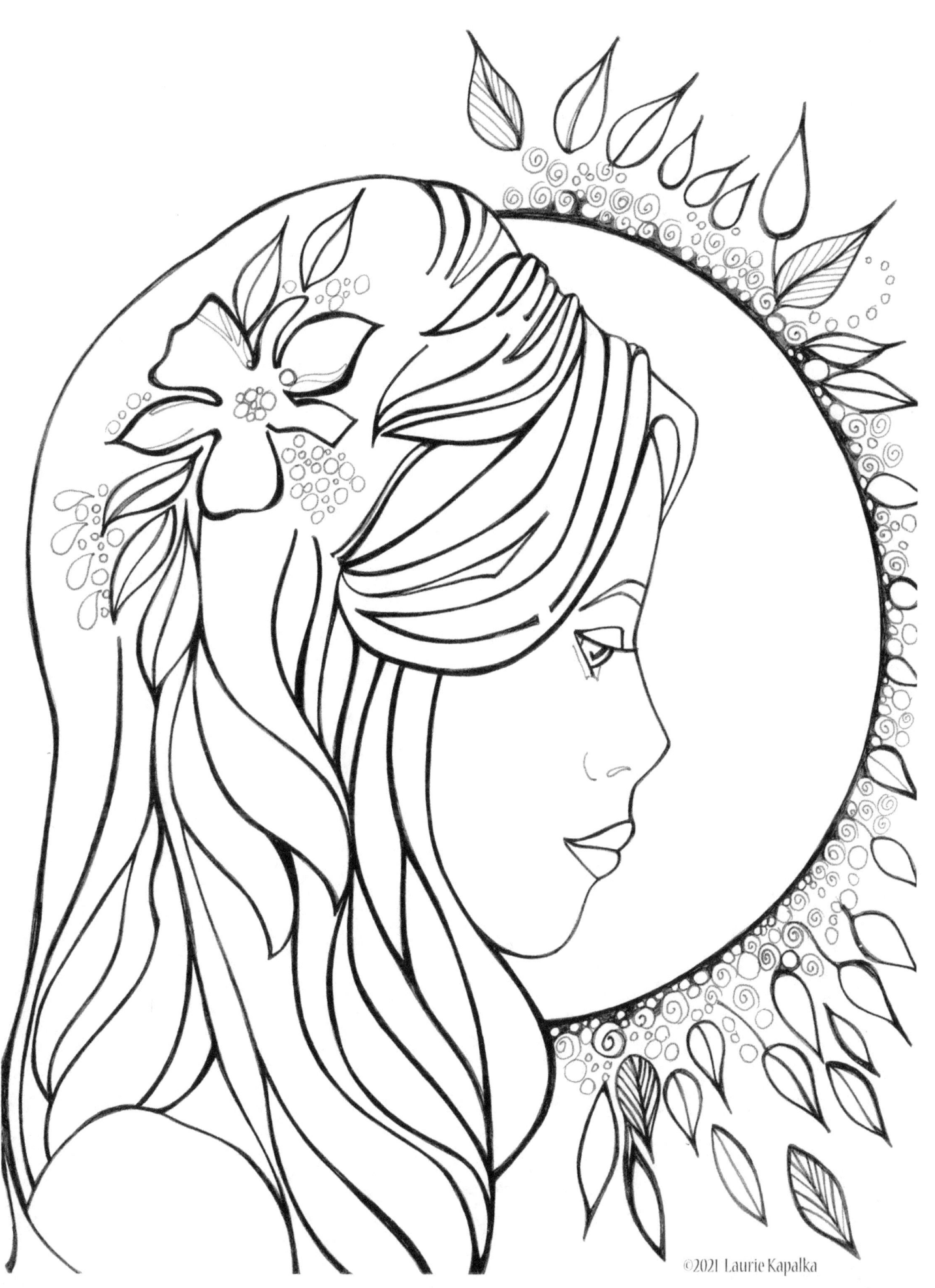

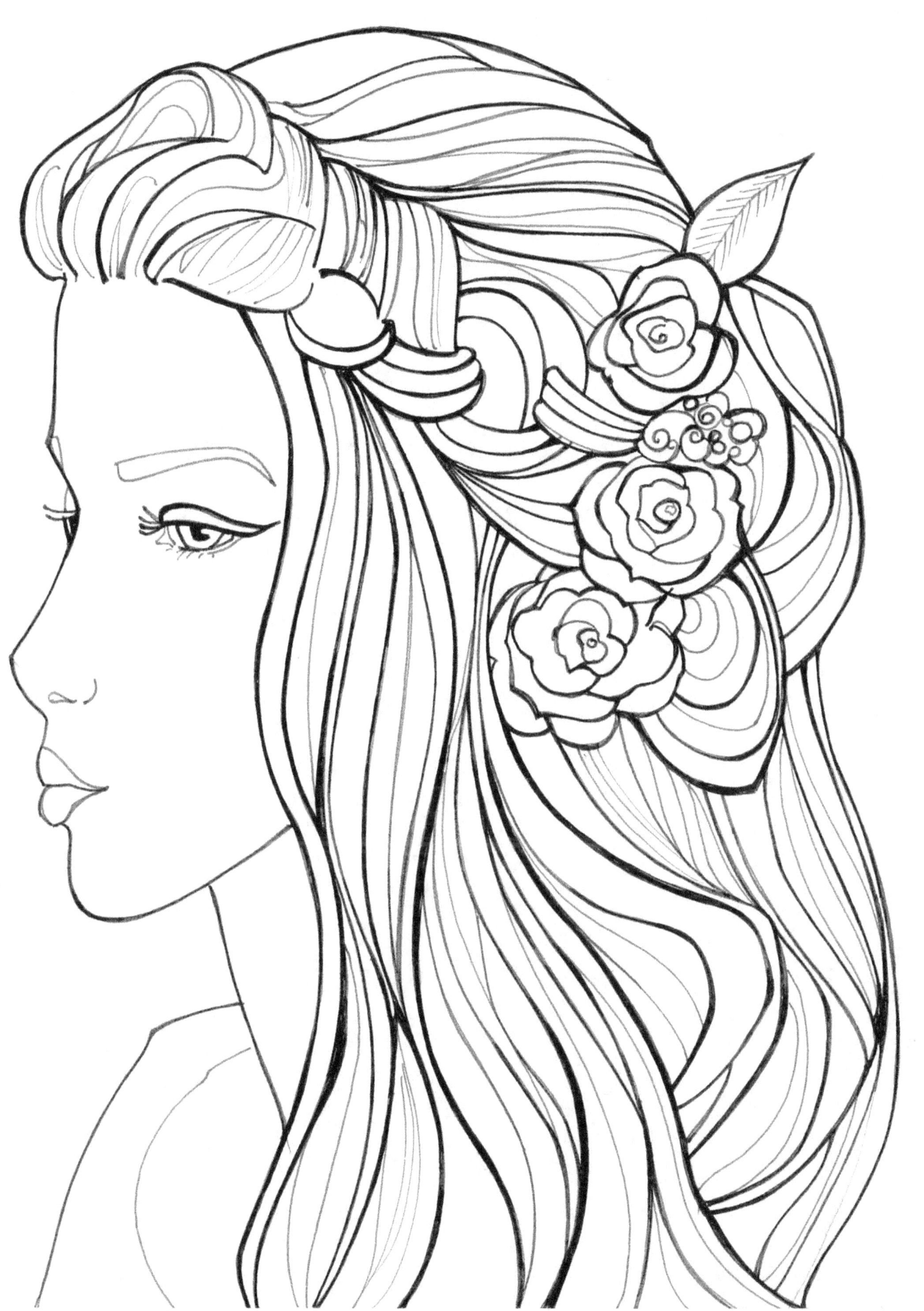

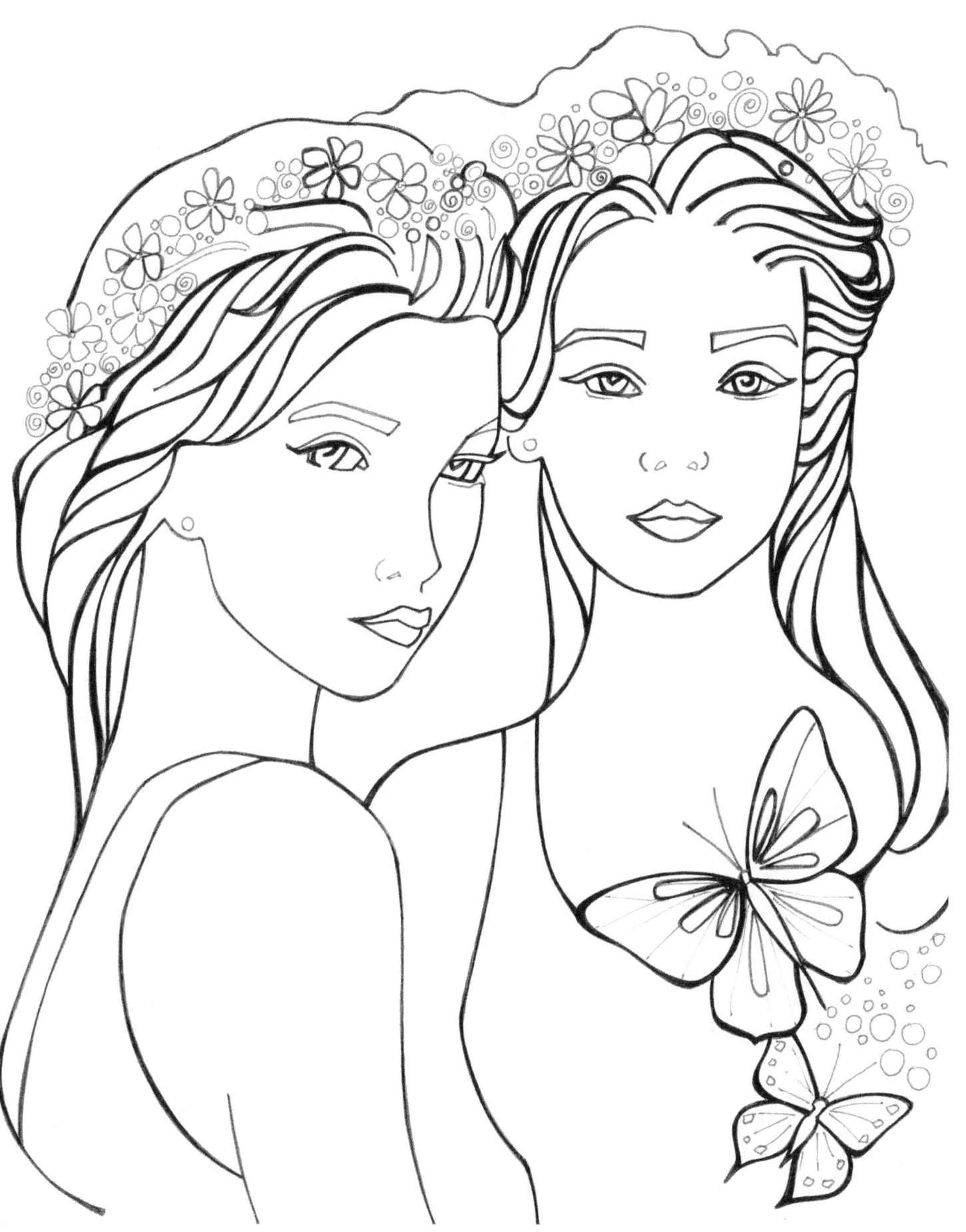

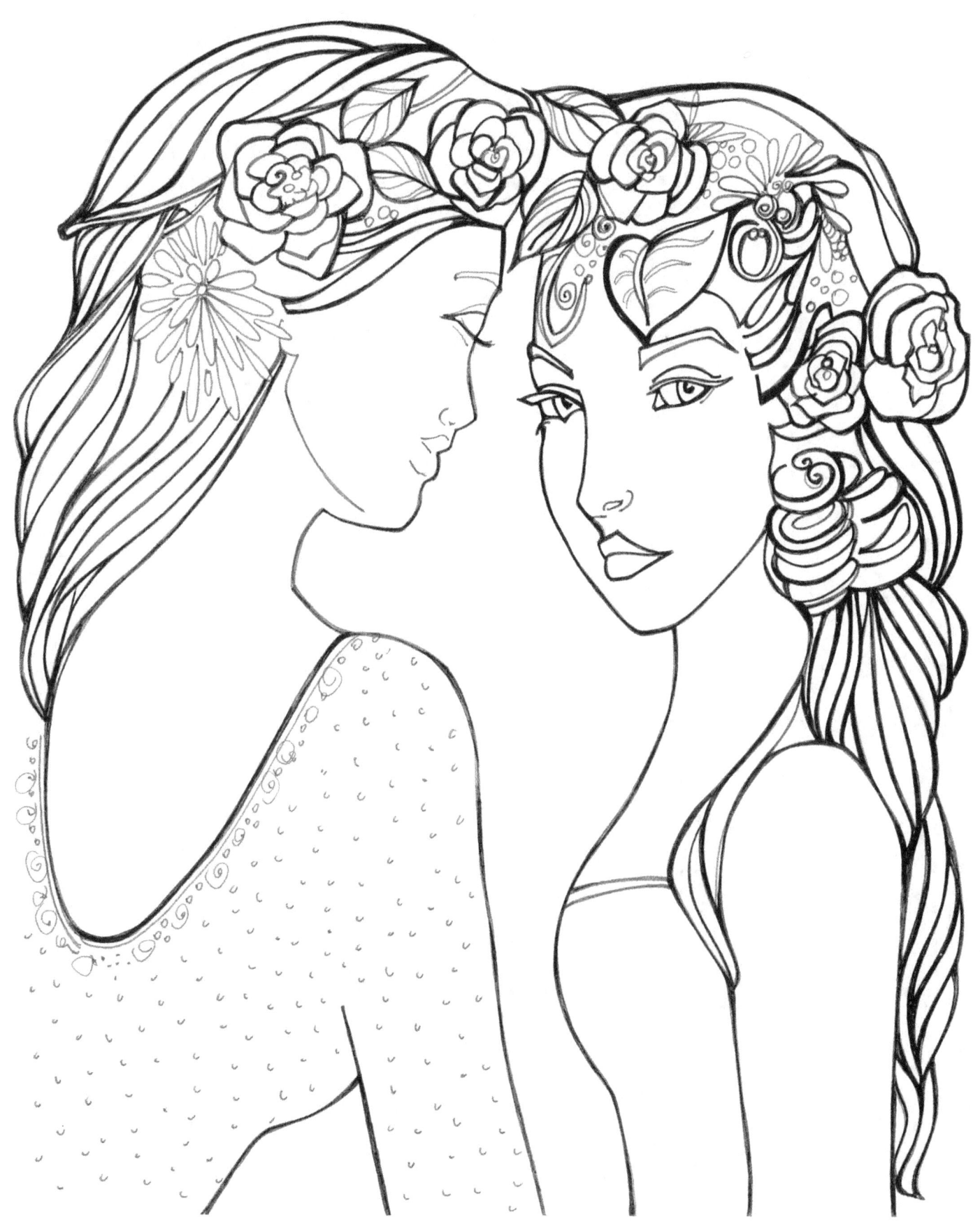

Color Test Sheet

www.ingramcontent.com/pod-product-compliance
Lightning Source LLC
Chambersburg PA
CBHW080523240526
45472CB00021BA/1911